OUT OF THIS WORLD

South West England

Edited by Donna Samworth

First published in Great Britain in 2015 by:

Young**Writers**

Remus House
Coltsfoot Drive
Peterborough
PE2 9BF
Telephone: 01733 890066
Website: www.youngwriters.co.uk

All Rights Reserved
Book Design by Ashley Janson
© Copyright Contributors 2015
SB ISBN 978-1-78443-883-8

Printed and bound in the UK by BookPrintingUK
Website: www.bookprintinguk.com

FOREWORD

Here at Young Writers our defining aim is to promote the joys of reading and writing to children and young adults and we are committed to nurturing the creative talents of the next generation. By allowing them to see their own work in print we believe their confidence and love of creative writing will grow.

Out Of This World is our latest fantastic competition, specifically designed to encourage the writing skills of primary school children through the medium of poetry. From the high quality of entries received, it is clear that it really captured the imagination of all involved.

We are proud to present the resulting collection of poems that we are sure will amuse and inspire.

An absorbing insight into the imagination and thoughts of the young, we hope you will agree that this fantastic anthology is one to delight the whole family again and again.

CONTENTS

Huish Primary School, Yeovil
Callum Hagreen (9) 1
Holly Parsons (10) 2
Tayla Moore 2
Marius Hall (9) 3
Harrison Caine (9) 3
Matthew Brooks (10) 4
Zak Nicholls (10) 5
Oscar Downing (10) 6
Erin Palmer (10) 6
Billy Bowditch (10) 7
Billy Woodham 7
Stuart Hillyar 8
Elliot Smith 8
Megan Salmon (9) 9
Sam Mellors (10) 9
Akanksha Das (10) 10
Owen Williams (10) 10
Daisy Snaith (10) 11
Madison Findlay (10) 11
Oliver George Castle (10) 12
Niamh O'Donnell (10) 12
Gracienne Haim (10) 13
Kiara Manley 13
Grace Palmer 14
James Mann (10) 14
Kalum Woolmington (10) 15
Imogen Nicholls (10) 15
Jemima Axe (10) 16
Daisy Mae Shire (9) 16
Robbie Christopher Hall (10) 17

Neroche Primary School, Ilminster
Abigail Dyer (9) 17
Charlie Lockyer (9) 18
Savannah Lamb (9) 19
Isla Grace Gibson (9) 20
Harriet Withers (10) 21
George Vickery (9) 22
Arthur Busby (9) 23
Felix Whereat (9) 24
Maia Jay (9) 25

Philip Honey (10) 26
George Souster (9) 27
Oliver Anthony Pugh Collins (9) 28
Holly Collins (10) 28
Edward Bidgood (9) 29
Olivia Wrenn (9) 30
Archie Spokes (9) 31
Oliver Clarke (10) 32
Finlay Roy Smith (9) 33
Tilly Wade (9) 34

Otterhampton Primary School, Bridgwater
Toby Smailes (10) 34
Poppy Dinah Mary Armstrong (11) 35
Sophie Austin (9) 36
Billy Scotting (8) 36
May Bruckel (10) 37
Harry Payne (11) 37
Freddy Perham (9) 38
Amelia Cadmore (10) 38
Olive Jean Maidment (10) 39
Abrianna Wood (11) 39
Rhys Smith (9) 40
Austin Doble (10) 40
Grace Bennett (11) 41
Henry Wood 41
Alexandra Mockridge (10) 42
Harry Philip Pyke (9) 42
Matthew Forrest (9) 42
Jack Shand (10) 43
Charlie Turner (9) 43
Tom Brooks (9) 43
Kieran James (9) 44
Sam Webber (9) 44
Amelia Chloe Abina Williams (9) 44
Oscar Stone (8) 45

St Aldhelm's CE(VA) Primary School, Shepton Mallet
Kitty Stone (9) 45
Trinity Hazel Piper Legresley (10) 46
Luke O'Brien (9) 46

Ayishah Parrott (10)	47
Daniel James (10)	47
Noah Robert Dowding Lees (8)	48
Cameron Fernandez McEwan (10)	48
Molly Connock (9)	49
Phoebe Evans (9)	49
George Milton-Parry (9)	50
Danniellé Pittard (9)	50
Grace Chapman (10)	51
Summer Kearn (9)	51
Alana Fiddy (8)	52
Archie Biggs (10)	52
Scarlett Way (8)	53
Charlotte Mary Pole (8)	53
George Robert Durston (9)	53
Georgia Moon (9)	54
Hayden Evans (8)	54
Libby Sawyer (9)	54
Jack Gilham (10)	55
Katherine Dyke (8)	55
Liam Kennedy (10)	55
Evie Ward (9)	56
Emma Witcombe (10)	56
Stefan Olindraru (8)	56
Billy Sheppard (8)	57
Lily-Mae Beatrice Sealey (10)	57
Lola Pittard (8)	57
Fern Nathan (9)	58
Jack Burgess (9)	58

St Andrew's CE(VA) Primary School, Weymouth

Amy Joanne Hunt (10)	59
Ruby Measures (10)	60
Bethan Phillips (10)	61

St Lawrence CE Primary School, Lechlade

Mae Rodia (9)	61
Tosca Knight (9)	62
Emily Tinney (10)	62
Isobel Parker (10)	63
Emily Coe (10)	63
Scarlett Rodia (9)	64
Campbell McDiarmid (10)	64
Aloula Goymer (9)	64
Esme Barlow (10)	65
Brooke Etty (10)	65

Olivia Peach (10)	65
Olivia Cripps (10)	66
Jago James (10)	66
Daniel Graham (10)	66

St Thomas More RC Primary School, Cheltenham

Owen Heaney (9)	67
Christopher Neale (9)	67
Kayla Young-Collins (9)	68
Brandon Njengah (9)	68
Kaitlyn Booth (10)	69
Joe Taylor (9)	69
Sonny Street (10)	70
McCauley Ayres (9)	70
Kay Mary Piper (10)	71
Riley Sibthorpe (10)	71
Emily Jayne Piper (10)	71

Stockland CE Primary Academy, Honiton

Katie Bartlett (9)	72
Phoebe Wakley	73
Isabella Corp-Hill (7)	73
Saffron Doble (7)	74
Jonathan Elliot Triner (8)	74
Liberty Wheeler (9)	75
Edie Martin (9)	75
Isaac Parris (7)	76
Phoebe Grace Lovell (9)	76
George Parris (9)	77
Sofia Corp-Hill (9)	77
Rose Moorman (7)	78
Thea Hawkins (8)	78
Tabitha Millington (7)	79
Maisy McCollum (8)	79
Minnie Zarri (10)	80
Anna Keen (10)	81
Kate Alexandra Cook (8)	82

Warden Hill Primary School, Cheltenham

Molly Ann Yasmin Young (10)	82
Ella Newman (7)	83
Sienna Viveash (10)	84
Becca Allen (9)	85
Faye James (10)	85
Sam Danson (10)	86

Jack Tomkins (9)	86
Kate Mitchell	87
Alwyne Adrian Williams (10)	87
Scarlett Gracie Cave (10)	88
Matthew Haines (10)	88
Daniel Edward Robertson (10)	89
Jack Nathan Pope (10)	89
Thomas Davies (10)	90
Bethany Browne (9)	90
Katherine Toner (9)	91
Antonio Bailey (9)	91
Millie Cunningham (9)	92
Laila Khaira (8)	92
Faith Warrington Alder (10)	93
Aamena Toufique Qureshi (10)	93
Rebecca Maughfling (10)	94
Zara Sharaf (9)	95
Sophie Miles (8)	96
Tabitha Murray-Birks (8)	96
Hannah Maughfling (8)	96
Taylor Ilott (9)	97
Edward Churchman (8)	98
Jessica Taylor (9)	98

Whipton Barton Federation, Exeter

Shenice Cooney (11)	99
Shelby Rose Tucker (11)	99
Cameron Thomas (11)	100
Alex Crane (11)	100
Hope Oldridge (11)	101
Lewis Moore (10)	101
Taylor Murphy (10)	102
Callum Harris (12)	102
Alicia Louise Farmer (10)	103
Louis Harry Watkiss (11)	103
David Hurford (11)	104
Charlie Helmann (11)	104
Brandon Martin (11)	105
Katie Mitchell (11)	105
Megan Reed (10)	106
Keira Lamerton (11)	106
Ryley Mortimore (11)	107
Corey Madge (10)	107
Adam Wilson (10)	108
Ellie-Mae Coles (11)	108
Lauren Sprague (11)	109

Eloise Taylor (11)	109
Emily Dunn (11)	110
Danielius Demjanovas (10)	110
Tomas Piskac (11)	111
Chloe Boyce (11)	111
Ben Turner (10)	112
Lillian Sharland (10)	112
Danny David Knight (11)	113
Lois Bennett (10)	113
Michaela Shapcott (11)	113
Conor Alsopp (10)	114
Mylie Freestone (11)	114
Coeinn Preston (10)	114
Ollie Blackmore (10)	115
Emanuel Krystian Kolbuszewski (10)	115
Chidera Melie (10)	115
Lila Rose Watkiss (9)	116
Michael Macleod (11)	116
Aaron Harry Brealey (10)	116
Yvette Louise Bogardis (10)	117
Oliver Purvis (9)	117
Luke Pring (11)	117
Reece Passmore (10)	118
Verity Jones Orr (10)	118
Ella Stone (10)	118
AJ Turner (10)	119
Tyriece Swift (9)	119
Nadia Thomas (10)	119
Kelsey Grinney (10)	120
Riley Smith (10)	120
Tj Smith (10)	120
Kasmira Swift (11)	121
Elysia Jade Kingdon (11)	121

Whitchurch Primary School, Tavistock

Alexandra Grace Ley (10)	121
Tal Pearson (6)	122
James Drew Waites (6)	122
Sheldon Blake Higgins	123
Sophie Mackenzie (10)	123
Niall (10)	123

THE POEMS

OUT OF THIS WORLD - South West England

Rescuing Russell

We found him on the roadside
Two Saturdays ago
He couldn't fly or even glide
He was a sad little crow.

We picked him up and held him
To see if he was hurt
But the light was very dim
But we could see he was alert.

We put him in our car
We took him to a park
He still couldn't fly very far
And by this time, it was getting dark.

We took him to our home
And we made a temporary cage
He was feeling quite alone
As he was squawking in a rage.

He thought we weren't very nice
Until we gave him food
We gave him cat food and rice
Now he's in a happy mood.

He sits upon my shoulder
And squawks right in my ear
I think I might be deaf
I really hope not, oh dear!

Maybe he'll visit one day
And bring his family too
I hope he knows the way
I wish you could meet him too.

Callum Hagreen (9)
Huish Primary School, Yeovil

The Unicorn's Journey

On Pluto there lived a unicorn
But he was lonely and cold.
He set off to find some heat and friends
Before he became too old.
He travelled to Neptune and Uranus
But they weren't quite his style.
Then he galloped around Saturn's rings
And that kept him happy for a while.
After, he explored huge Jupiter
But there were no unicorns there.
So he carried on to Mars
Which was also barren and bare.
He made friends with the horses on Earth
Who gave him a clue where to go.
'Unicorns like it really hot,
They're nearer the sun you know!'
He stopped briefly on Venus to rest
For he knew his journey was near an end.
Finally, he arrived on Mercury
Where he met his new unicorn friends.
Happily he galloped around
Enjoying his new friends and the heat.
The sun restored their powers
From their horns to their feet!

Holly Parsons (10)
Huish Primary School, Yeovil

Congratulations your poem has been chosen as the best in this book!

The Sun

B urns like your soul after a curse
R ings the Earth like a swingball
I lluminated like the lights of a disco
G igantic like a balloon about to pop
H ot, like a scorching stove
T ippy-toe, to get high in the sky.

Tayla Moore
Huish Primary School, Yeovil

OUT OF THIS WORLD - South West England

My Favourite Planets

Venus, the hot planet
Can reach 460 degrees
Named after the Roman god of love
It's the second planet from the sun

Mars, the red planet
Made of ice and rust
It is the closest planet to Earth
And is the next step of space travel

Jupiter, the biggest planet
Is a great gas giant
It has 67 moons
Most of which are extremely big

Saturn, the other gas giant
With 62 moons
It has mesmerising rings
And could float in water

Neptune, the cloudy planet
Has the largest cloud of all
It is the eighth from the sun
And is very, very cold.

Marius Hall (9)
Huish Primary School, Yeovil

My Cat Mittens

M y kitten, Mittens, is so cuddly and cute
I n the house she runs round after her sister, Boots
T he cat inside her is loving and fluffy
T his cat is really adorable when she comes in and cuddles me
E very day she goes out and hunts for birds and rats
N ever does she bite me but I bet she wants to bite other cats
S he means so much to me, I love her and I know she loves me.

Harrison Caine (9)
Huish Primary School, Yeovil

Minecraft Hobbies

You could go adventuring, mining, brewing
You could find some diamonds, diamonds, diamonds
You could brew some potions, potions, potions
And find any biome!

You could fight some creepers, zombies, spiders
And some skeletons, witches
And Endermen
And get their loots.

You could find a village
With all the villagers
And be rich with shiny emeralds
Or lots of other things.

You could got to the Nether
And fight the Wither
Or go to the End
And fight the Ender Dragon.

You can build a roller coaster or a skyscraper
Or anything you want
Let your imagination flow
Because it's up to you.

Matthew Brooks (10)
Huish Primary School, Yeovil

When I Met Harry Potter

When I met Harry Potter
I met him on an adventure
And we both entered the Triwizard tournament
Harry didn't get through because he fell off Hogwarts tower.

I faced a fierce dragon
The dragon's breath was a lot hotter than I expected
Its breath was hot lava
I got its egg by knocking it out.

The second task came
And I was so surprised
When I had to swim
I saw my friends underwater so I rescued them.

I won, which amazed me
And I would hate it if we had to do it again
That was the scariest moment of my life
I celebrated with all my friends when I got back.

The next day I went home
But before I did I said goodbye
And took home the trophy
For winning the tournament.

Zak Nicholls (10)
Huish Primary School, Yeovil

Delilah Waggington

That big brown bear that roams my house
Bigger than a pig, quieter than a mouse
A tongue so long, it causes a drought
In her water bowl, day in, day out
She is a Wheaten
On cuteness never to be beaten
She will demolish her food
Faster than you ever could
Her nose is blacker than coal
Blacker than the blackest black hole
Her fur is so bountiful, so soft, so strokeable
That's why she is so big and so lovable
Her tail is a barometer
It indicates her mood
When up it creates a windy, waggy storm
When down and still
It gives me a sudden chill
As this barely ever happens
Nevertheless it is always curled
My dog, Delilah, is out of this world.

Oscar Downing (10)
Huish Primary School, Yeovil

What's An Alien?

Will an alien be my friend or drive me round the bend?
Are they red and do they have two heads?
Are they yellow? Maybe they're jello.
Are they pink? At least I think.
Are they green or do they gleam?
Are they blue or do they leave any clues?
Are they violet or do they have spacecraft pilots?
Are they grey or do they come down to play?
Are they funny? Will they make me grin?
Or will they leave a tingle on my skin?

Erin Palmer (10)
Huish Primary School, Yeovil

OUT OF THIS WORLD - South West England

PGL Adventure!

Osmington is nearly here when we board the bus,
And we all give a cheer,
Butterflies inside my tum,
Excited, nervous but I'm sure it'll be fun.
In a room with my mates,
I just know it'll be great,
On the beach digging sand,
Pebble art and seaweed found.
Lots of lovely food to eat,
My favourite is lots of meat,
Giant leap off of the tower,
Abseiling, zipwire, even in a heavy shower.
Dragonboat racing, lots of fun,
And on the coach for Portsmouth sun,
The week whizzing by,
Ready for bed, we all give a sigh.
The last day is here and ready to pack,
Tidy my cabin and gather my rucksack,
Time to go home, back in my bed,
Ready to rest my head.

Billy Bowditch (10)
Huish Primary School, Yeovil

Penguins

I have always loved penguins, I cannot tell you why,
But I think it is because I saw one glide beneath the frozen sky.

I stood and watched the penguins waddling around,
Always looking out for each other, hardly making a sound.

Penguins to me are like the kings of the sea,
Rushing through the water like a torpedo in the sky.

They have such fluffy feathers, usually black and white,
But sometimes some have a special yellow stripe.

Billy Woodham
Huish Primary School, Yeovil

Minecraft

Minecraft is a game
That people love to play

Mining blocks
Breaking through rocks

You can play it single
Or multi-player
But it's better if you play with two

You should never mine down
Or you might drown
In a pool of hot lava

Monsters come out at night
To give you quite a fright

Build a house
It could be a dirt house

Minecraft is a fun game to play
That everybody loves to play.

Stuart Hillyar
Huish Primary School, Yeovil

Superheroes

I am a superhero, brave and bold
I save citizens, young and old.

Superheroes wear a cape and a cowl
When we save the world wolves will howl.

All super villains are mean and cruel
But all they want to do is rule, rule, rule!

People on Earth like to see me whizz by
Sometimes they see me flying sky high.

All villains make a collision
But I will see them with my X-ray vision.

Elliot Smith
Huish Primary School, Yeovil

Earth Is My Home

I am a little girl and Earth is my home
I live on land and swim in the sea
Earth moves around the sun
Which gives us day and is bright
And has one large moon which gives us night
At night in the sky the stars twinkle and glow
They make shapes and patterns for us to know
And when the sun rises they all disappear
A start of a new day all shiny and clear
Sometimes clouds cross the sky
That may burst to give rain
To feed the plants and grain
In some dry countries it helps the drought
So the people and animals can continue to live
I would love to travel to outer space
I know it would be such an interesting place
But for now I must live here on Earth
To be with my family and all those I love.

Megan Salmon (9)
Huish Primary School, Yeovil

Thunderbirds

Thunderbirds are *go!*
What an amazing TV show.

Tracy Island is where they live
All their time to save the world they give.

Ships 1, 2, 3, 4 and 5
Thunderbirds are alive.

Stunning speeds they fly
Through the clouds in the sky.

Trying to catch the Evil Hood
So that they keep the world good.

Sam Mellors (10)
Huish Primary School, Yeovil

Wagga Wagga Woo

I have got this pet . . .
It is called a Wagga Wagga Woo
It has a fluffy tail of a bunny,
And scaly dragon wings too!
It has a dog's tail and body;
And big blue eyes.
It is really a stubborn creature,
And rather stupid too -
When you ask him a question
He hasn't got a clue!
He is heavy as a rock
And can give vicious looks!
He lounges around the sitting room,
And he chews on Mum's books.
He is the best pet ever
My Wagga Wagga Woo . . .
Even though he is grumpy
He loves me back too!

Akanksha Das (10)
Huish Primary School, Yeovil

Marvin The Dog

Marvin is my best friend
With him a lot of the time I spend
He sits with me, we watch TV
He's not allowed but thinks he's human you see
He wiggles his bum and wags his tail
And never chews up the mail
He likes to run and chase the birds
And when we're not looking, sneaks up the stairs
He can be naughty from time to time
But I love him lots
That's why I made this rhyme.

Owen Williams (10)
Huish Primary School, Yeovil

Hetty

Foundling Hetty,
Just a foundling girl.
Abandoned by Ma,
Poor little Hetty.

Hetty Feather,
The name they gave her.
At the hospital,
Just for foundlings.

Smart and clever,
She should know better.
But that's not the case,
Naughty Hetty!

Fiery hair,
Freckles on her face.
Eyes blue like the sky,
This is Hetty.

Daisy Snaith (10)
Huish Primary School, Yeovil

Remembering Feelings

At night I think about my feelings,
Feelings from throughout the day,
Or looking back a longer way.
Sometimes my feelings are happy,
Sometimes my feelings make me want to cry,
Sometimes my feelings are stressed,
I feel like I need to be calm.
And when my feelings are hurt,
I feel I need some love,
I reach out my arm for Teddy,
Snuggle him close to me.
And I fall asleep,
Because he's always been there for me.

Madison Findlay (10)
Huish Primary School, Yeovil

Planets Of The Solar System

We live in a galaxy,
With planets so far away,
But all these planets are special,
And are here to stay.

Half of the planets are,
Mercury, Venus, Earth and Mars,
But Mars seems to be named
After one of the chocolate bars.

Another half are,
Jupiter, Saturn, Uranus and Neptune,
But if you were to go to Neptune,
You'd turn into a shrivelled prune.

We live in a galaxy,
With planets so far away,
But all these planets are special,
And are here to stay.

Oliver George Castle (10)
Huish Primary School, Yeovil

The Ten

The symbolic sign of the gods, the scorching fiery ball.
The moonless miniature Minotaur racing around the track, all it takes is 88 laps.
The very first of the twins, the hottest of the nine, this twin is a vicious vulture . . .
And this one is an exotic eagle, the exciting life form exists only here.
The magical mermaids swim around in the mysterious red sea.
It's the nearest one that we can see.
Japanese giants roam the big red spot, in our sky it's only a dot.
The solar system's ringmaster, it's the Lord of the Rings.
The unusual unicorn spinning on its side, tap-dancing as it goes by.
The naughty narwhals with 14 round horns.
Mickey's dwarf dog.

Niamh O'Donnell (10)
Huish Primary School, Yeovil

OUT OF THIS WORLD - South West England

A Trip Into Space!

Boarding our rocket for an adventure around space,
You can come too, it's going to be ace!
First we can see magical Mercury, it's planet number one,
Closest to the sun.
Next is Venus, it's the hottest planet of them all,
That's 460°C squished up into a ball!
Now here comes Earth, we've seen it before,
It looks perfect from here, but it's full of war.
Then there's Mars, it's extremely old,
Do take a coat, it's also cold!
Look, it's Jupiter with 107 known moons,
All dotted around like a bunch of balloons!
Now in the distance what can you see?
Oh, it's Saturn, famously known for being seen by you and me!
But now it's time to go as our trip has ended,
Though the time we had together, well it was just splendid!

Gracienne Haim (10)
Huish Primary School, Yeovil

Space

Neil Armstrong flew up in a rocket
He went as high as the sky
With a chain in his pocket
As he flew in his rocket.

Space was as dark as coal
The planets were untold
But the moon was bright
And the rocket was in flight
As the planets twirled round and round.

The stars flickered and bickered
Shooting stars flying past and out of the Milky Way
A meteorite flew past as bright as gold
It matched the gold on Armstrong's chain.

Kiara Manley
Huish Primary School, Yeovil

Somewhere Out There

Somewhere out there,
There is a world that has been painted,
Painted black with a paintbrush.
Somewhere in that world,
There are fascinating balls of fire,
Floating miraculously in that world.
Somewhere in that place,
There is a queen,
A queen ball of fire that rules over the rest.
Somewhere in that amazing world,
There are eight spheres that circle the queen,
Each a different world.
We live on one of those spheres.
Somewhere out there is a world,
A world of wonders and breathtaking beauty
And this world is in our solar system.

Grace Palmer
Huish Primary School, Yeovil

One Way Trip

Although there's no gravity in space
On Mars we'll create a colony
The money we spend won't be a waste
But instead go down in history

Despite the fact that it's a one-way ticket
It would be a thrilling trip
And the iron there, we could mine it, use it!
So let's start building our rocket ship!

Now the rocket's built, let us pack our things
Let's get on our way, up to the stars
Let's say goodbye to Earth and its belongings
Because now we're in a rocket on a journey to Mars.

James Mann (10)
Huish Primary School, Yeovil

OUT OF THIS WORLD - South West England

Mars Lander Adventure

I am going on a great adventure,
I am going to outer space,
The rocket is fully loaded,
And there isn't much space!

I am sitting at the controls,
The countdown has just started, 5, 4, 3, 2, 1 . . .
The journey has just begun,
The rocket shakes and rattles as it heads towards the stars,
The Earth is getting smaller as we reach for the stars,
Zoom goes the rocket, past the moon and heads towards Mars.

The journey's almost over, Mars is in sight,
The rocket touches down on the crumbly, red surface,
We jump out of our rocket and continue our adventure,
Being the first people and there are aliens in our rocket!

Kalum Woolmington (10)
Huish Primary School, Yeovil

Space

The other day I went to space
To see if I could find an alien race.
But all I found were planets and stars
I just have to tell you that I saw Mars.

The other day I went to Mars
I saw the Milky Way not Milky Bars.
All of a sudden I took a trip
Now I am on a rocket ship.

The other day I explored a rocket ship
All of a sudden the rocket took a trip.
Then I saw an asteroid belt
Then the rocket I was on began to melt.

Imogen Nicholls (10)
Huish Primary School, Yeovil

Dancing Dolphins

As I lie down beside the sea,
I always wonder if I'm going to see my friends.
Slowly, I watch the sun slip behind the sea,
Far away in the distance.

I glance at the sea,
And a beautiful dolphin appears.
As it dances in and out of the waves,
It looks like an energetic soloist in a ballet performance.

Its sparkly blue skin twinkles in the sunlight,
I feel I'm in a fairy tale.
As I stare there's one thing in my head,
How I wish to be a dancing dolphin.

Jemima Axe (10)
Huish Primary School, Yeovil

Roller Coasters

As I took my seat on the Exhilarater,
They strapped me in to keep me safe.
My excitement started bubbling up,
The ride began and it felt like I was heading to the sky.
My heart was beating with fear,
As the drop came near.
Then *whoosh*, down we went with a scream,
And my hands in the air.
The camera flashed as we went round again,
I had the same thrilling feeling although,
I knew the ride was coming to an end!

Daisy Mae Shire (9)
Huish Primary School, Yeovil

OUT OF THIS WORLD - South West England

Fish, Fish, Fish

Fishing is my hobby, I think it is fun
And if I had my way, I would fish all day long!
The fishing tackle I have is a rod, reel, line, weight
And a hook which holds my bait.
The fish that I have caught are carp, bass, bream, rudd
And I would like to catch a chubb.
A 19lb carp is my PB (personal best)
Now I am waiting for a 26lb guest.
Fish on . . .

Robbie Christopher Hall (10)
Huish Primary School, Yeovil

Futuristic Fairies

Once there was a dainty doll's house,
In a necessary, noisy nursery.
There lived several gorgeous,
Stunning, pocket-sized toy fairies.
The doll's house was painted
Pearl-pink with spectacular, vivid windows,
As well as a luminous front door with a petite handle,
And a garden with beautiful tulips,
Amongst the hedges.
There was a fantastic fairy called Chloe,
A lovely, caring one called Rosie,
And a beautiful, friendly fairy called Grace.
They had just arrived.
Grace opened the dazzling, bright front door
As they danced inside,
Leaving Rosie with all the luggage.
They skipped across carpet
Like stepping stones along a river.
Grace opened the crystal-clear fridge door
To look inside for a feast,
Took out silver iced buns with pearls dotted around.

Abigail Dyer (9)
Neroche Primary School, Ilminster

Out Of This World

Come and join us in outer space,
Where all our dreams meet and greet,
Where all the stars twinkle brightly,
Where planets collide and say, 'Hello.'

Come and join us in outer space,
Where we fly to Mercury in our crystal ruby rockets,
To explore what lies beyond,
Red dust everywhere, nothing could live on this boiling hot planet,
Not even in a metal spacesuit.

Come and join us in outer space,
Whilst we fly to Mars, the red planet,
We land to see an underground race of Martians,
We go to say hello but all they do is babble,
So we climb up the ladder and blast off . . .

Come and join us in outer space,
When we land on Saturn's rings,
Where the most famous rings are made,
And sent down to Earth in little boxes to help happy couples,
So back to our spaceship to explore more.

Come and join us in outer space,
Where we explore Pluto,
The coldest planet in our solar system,
We'll need super-heated suits to survive this one,
So I think we should skip this one.

Come and join us in outer space,
Where we move onto planet G,
Little is known about this planet,
As it is not in our solar system,
Everything is silent down below,
Where the wind doesn't even blow.
So I don't know about you,
But this one might have been abandoned . . .
So back to our rocket where we're going home.

Charlie Lockyer (9)
Neroche Primary School, Ilminster

Aquamarine Horses

Pretty Pegasus,
Cute flying horses in the sky.
Aquamarine horse.

Velvety, silky,
Pegasus are charming.
Aquamarine horse.

Obliging, lovely,
I love any Pegasus.
Aquamarine horse.

Cute Pegasus,
Pegasus everywhere.
Aquamarine horse.

Tender-hearted, kind,
They're as fine as anything.
Aquamarine horse.

Beautiful, charming,
Amazing sights in the world.
Silky, cute, kind horse.

Cobalt, attractive,
Cerulean, nice Pegasus.
Silky, cute, kind horse.

Charismatic horse,
Pleasing, spotty, flying things.
Silky, cute, kind horse.

A breed of horses,
So kind, cuddly and calm.
Silky, cute, kind horse.

Sensible horses,
Most of the time they're funny.
Silky, cute, kind horse.

Savannah Lamb (9)
Neroche Primary School, Ilminster

The Queen's Loo!

My cousin, Lewis, sat on the Queen's loo the other day,
But something went wrong to his dismay!
For the posh loo would not flush,
His cry, 'Argh!' made him blush!

The Queen was listening from outside,
'Lewis, are you sure you're alright?'
This made his heart freeze with fright,
He had to do something quick,
Otherwise off with his head and on his thigh a kick.

The Queen said, 'I'm coming in, wait till you see, now run along
Lewis, run along for me!'
Lewis' muscles froze,
But this was no time to doze!
He ran to a cupboard under the sink,
Even if he made a sudden clink,
He would be found in a bubble of trouble!
But oh no! The toilet roll fell off the dispenser,
Things were now getting ten times tenser!

He picked it up and rushed back to where he was before,
But now faster by a split second or more,
Although Queenie only wanted to see if he was alright!
Which thawed his heart leaving no more fright.
He thought he was in love!
With her hair as soft as the sun from up above!

'Come on Lewis, let's go have some tea!'
Lewis added, 'With honey fresh from the bees!'
The Queen said, 'With scones, crumpets, muffins and bread,
Then I can fill my empty head!'
So the two of them went off and now our story ends,
I hope you can remember this story about them being best friends!

Isla Grace Gibson (9)
Neroche Primary School, Ilminster

Errrr There's A Bug!

Errr there's a bug!
It's as small as a microscope.
It's a flea!
OMG, it's shouting, 'Weeee!'
I can't believe it.

Errr there's a bug!
Swiftly scuttling across the floor.
It's a beetle!
That was stuck in tacky treacle!
I can't believe it!

Errr there's a bug!
Compact like a chocolate bar.
It's ants.
And they're wearing pants.
I can't believe it!

Errr there's a bug!
All different colours, red and white.
It's a ladybird!
Licking the lemon curd!
I can't believe it!

How many bugs did I see today?
A flea shouting.
A beetle in treacle.
Ants in pants.
A ladybird licking lemon curd.
I can't believe it!
Bugs are creepy.
But I like them in every way!

Harriet Withers (10)
Neroche Primary School, Ilminster

The Battle For The World

Millions and millions of miles below Earth
There lives a fire world and a fire lord
There also lives a water world and a water lord
They all have cannons, walls, soldiers, weapons, archers.

The water army and the fire army both set off for war
The fire archers started shooting shiny fire arrows
Then the water soldiers started shooting sapphire blue cannons
They all held up their glistening deadly shields.

The water and fire soldiers clashed their fire and water swords
The fire army get out their cyclops and killed one hundred men
But then the water army let go of their spiders
Then killed one hundred men, the cyclops and spiders are dead.

The water soldiers shoot their arrows
The fire soldiers shoot their deadly cannons
The water 2,000 men dig underground
Then break the dark floor below the fire army.

The shiny water army get back up
The fire lord sent 200 men on horses to attack
All of the troops died and 200 water men died too
The water and fire archers shoot arrows and hold up their shields.

The fire and water army shot them with black-as-night cannon balls
Both of the lords stepped out then clashed water and fire swords
The water lord cuts the helmet of the fire lord
He stabs his sword in him and puts his helmet on his sword.

The gleaming water army killed all of the 1,799 fire army men
The water army break their walls
They all now live in peace.

George Vickery (9)
Neroche Primary School, Ilminster

OUT OF THIS WORLD - South West England

The Green Marshmallow That Thinks He's A Cloud

Once upon a time
There was a luminous
Bright green, happy cloud.

He planned to go on
Holiday to the sun
As yellow as fire and gold.

But then he realised
He was as slow as a snail
But he still set off!

It took as long
As the beautiful world
To get to the huge sun.

He slithered to the
Yellow sun that is up high
He got to the sun!

He forgot that he
Was a marshmallow
So he got very burnt!

His mother came back
She wasn't very happy
So she smacked his bum!

Arthur Busby (9)
Neroche Primary School, Ilminster

The Mysterious Planet

On a planet far, far away,
There lives a small cosy hut which looks like a nut,
And in that hut there lives an alien called Zob,
Zob likes to zoom at a hundred miles an hour,
Under the beautiful night sky.

On a stormy horrible night, there was a bit of a fright,
When Zob's engine was going *snap, crackle, pop*,
He needed to go to the shop,
But instead he went *bing, bang, bonk* and fell to the ground.

He landed on a planet,
One he'd never seen before,
Then suddenly the night started becoming light,
It was brilliant, amazing, extraordinary.

There was a puma eating tuna,
A pig in a wig and a bat in a hat,
It was the best thing he'd ever seen.

He saw something in the distance,
It was a shiny, tiny thing,
It was a spaceship,
It was his.

Zob's ship was now a clean machine,
He hopped into it and zoomed home.

Felix Whereat (9)
Neroche Primary School, Ilminster

OUT OF THIS WORLD - South West England

Jelly Bean Land

Bouncing along on a big, ruby-red space hopper,
Was a little girl called Rose.
One day when she was bouncing,
She realised that the space hopper
Was shaped as a jelly bean.
She found a big, long trail of them,
So she followed them.
But then she realised,
That she was not at home anymore.
Rose didn't know where she was,
Until a big queen made out of jelly beans
Plodded along.
And then she realised that everything was
Made out of jelly beans.
The trees were,
The grass was,
And even the houses were.
Just then Rose saw the queen eating grass.
Because she was eating the grass,
Rose started to eat the grass.
Rose loved it there!
She said it was the best time of her life!
It was marvellous.
So remember, always like jelly beans.

Maia Jay (9)
Neroche Primary School, Ilminster

The World Of Terraria

Once, there was an island called Terraria.
To most people, The Lost Island.
I'll tell you why.
There are creatures of unknown (most of them are blood-thirsty monsters).
But some creatures are weird, harmless.
There are two monsters, one of a kind
And the most destructive.

One of them is part snake and part human . . .
It's Medusa.
Her hair was born by Pandora's box,
It used all its dark and demonic evil on Medusa
And cursed her for eternity!
If anything lays eyes on her,
You turn to stone forever,
So the only way to see her face is the reflection of a mirror.
Even her hair is deadly pythons.

Next one is a dragon
That really has a terrible sneer.
It's the Hydra . . .
It says if you cut off one of their heads,
Two more come and replace the dead one!

Philip Honey (10)
Neroche Primary School, Ilminster

OUT OF THIS WORLD - South West England

Scrumdiddlyumptious

Once long ago, there was a great surprise!
In the glistening, sparkling moonlight.
Will we ever know what happens next?
Listen in to find out.
When a girl was in her bed,
Something magical was right ahead.

What was it, in the light?
It gave her a terrible fright.
Why was she frightened?
I'll never know,
Maybe it was 'cause of the gentle glow.

She headed towards it,
To find out more but what next was a sensational shock.
Scrummy candy all around,
Stuffing her face while she gets the chance.

Frantically rushing all around, trying to get candy before she can't,
She needs to hurry up before her time is up,
Otherwise, she goes home without any luck.
She sees the glow again,
What does she choose?
Of course, it's home she will always do.

George Souster (9)
Neroche Primary School, Ilminster

The End Of The School Day

It's the end of the school day
The children say hooray
As they zoom through the school gate.
Fred said, 'Hey, come and play!'
So Bob ran to the park.
Rolling in the muddy and slushy mud,
He said to his friend who was stuck,
'Oh dear, how are you going to get out of the brown mud?'
'I don't know but let's have a nice, friendly chat.'
When they got out,
They went to Bob's house,
And for a surprise,
Fred's mum was waiting, having pie!
Fred said to his mum,
Who was saying goodbye,
'I don't want to go to school,
Because it's boring and I'm snoring!'
'OK dear, only for one year,
If you promise to do the dishes every day!'

Oliver Anthony Pugh Collins (9)
Neroche Primary School, Ilminster

A Lovely Night

Shimmer of moonlight,
Sparkling out to the night,
Stars glowing so bright.

Its glorious colours,
Glistening in the midnight sky,
We watched in delight.

It lights up the sky,
Like the Northern Lights in delight,
Never forget this!

Holly Collins (10)
Neroche Primary School, Ilminster

Half A Planet Each

Out of our world,
Over a million miles away,
There's a planet,
That has aliens that don't like each other,
So they split it in half.

Out of our world,
Even more miles away,
There's a planet,
Where both aliens like art,
One side scribbles and
The other likes pointillism.

Out of our world,
About 50,000 miles away,
There's a small planet,
That likes sport,
The side on the left,
Likes cricket,
And the right loves football!

Edward Bidgood (9)
Neroche Primary School, Ilminster

Above The Heavens

One day above the heavens,
Love, mythical creatures and magic were invented,
And rainbows covered the sky,
It's a happy place, not miserable,
You will never see any creature cry.

But there weren't just joyful creatures,
There were evil unicorns!
Which are enemies to the stunning creatures.
The evil unicorns were black, black as midnight.
They hid in caves and grabbed anything that came by.

The next day, the queen counted the creatures.
There usually were 1,000,000
But there were only 500,000.
All the mythical creatures thought they were ill.
But no, they had been captured by the enemies,
The evil unicorns!
The mythical creatures were worried
That they would be next!

Olivia Wrenn (9)
Neroche Primary School, Ilminster

The Mad Match

Magical Messi
Passed the deadly defenders
And beats the keeper.

And it hits the net
'Goal!' says the commentator
The crowd goes crazy.

Real Madrid kick-off
Rubbish Ronaldo trips up
Barcelona laugh.

Pepe goes crazy
He runs at Neymar and screams
Then Suárez bites him.

Pepe falls over
And, in pain, punches the ground
He screams at Suárez.

Archie Spokes (9)
Neroche Primary School, Ilminster

Nanny Goes Boom

There's a nanny called Poppy,
She's always hungry, always demanding food
Her husband is getting frustrated,
He says, 'Nanny you'll go boom soon.'

When Poppy's husband doesn't give her food,
She starts to go crazy!
Starts getting in a mood.

Eventually he gives her food,
Without thinking, Poppy eats it all in one.
She's in a better mood.

One night she had a dream,
There was loads of giant food,
Telling her not to eat another piece.
Poppy didn't listen,
Poppy went *boom!*

Oliver Clarke (10)
Neroche Primary School, Ilminster

OUT OF THIS WORLD - South West England

Chelsea Football Club

Chelsea FC, a footballer's dream
Better than Arsenal
And Man City
They'll never stop scoring
Home or away.

Chelsea FC, a footballer's dream
They could play with their eyes closed
Still beating every team.

Chelsea FC, a footballer's dream
With Drogba, Hazard and Costa too
Slipping through the defence
In training too.

Chelsea FC, a footballer's dream
Screaming fans
Becoming a true blue.

Finlay Roy Smith (9)
Neroche Primary School, Ilminster

Scrumptious Dream Land

Far, far away,
Tucked away in the luscious, white snow,
There stands Scrumptious Dream Land!
Only good girls and boys go there.
If you decide to mess around,
You get sent to murky Mars
By the evil Candy King!
I will let you into a huge secret,
Only one girl got sent to murky Mars!
Back to the story.
There are scrumptious candy canes,
Swinging on the green tree branches.
There is edible grass!
And you can eat the trees.
Remember, only good girls and boys go!

Tilly Wade (9)
Neroche Primary School, Ilminster

Moon Landing

Countdown starting,
Rockets blasting,
Ground shaking,
Smoke pouring,
Rocket lifting
Crowd cheering,
Fumes disappearing,
Earth shrinking,
Rocket dismantling,
Apollo disappearing,
Moon growing,
Engines stopping,
Legs growing,
Control room cheering,
Apollo landing.

Toby Smailes (10)
Otterhampton Primary School, Bridgwater

Stare Into Space (SIS)

I may only look like an ordinary person,
Well, an ordinary girl.
But I've got a talent,
That could change the world!
I like to look out the window,
Well, stare out into space,
With my eyes totally stuck,
Just like a glaze!
I look up to the stars,
Glittering and shining in the sky,
Up where even the clouds don't
Dare to fly.
I get a glimpse of all the planets,
Mercury, Pluto and Mars.
But I wish that I could lunge,
And jump onto that shooting star!
I can see the aliens laughing and playing football,
Looks like Upthrust has taken the goal.
Sometimes I see a giant, turning doughnut,
Wait, that's a black hole!
Even though I'm short-sighted,
And I can see the universe and atmosphere,
I can barely see five metres away,
But to me the galaxies are crystal clear,
The sky looks sewn,
Like a glistening colony.
I guess that's why,
They call it astronomy.
But there's just one dream I wish to dare,
That I'd have more than just views from up there!

Poppy Dinah Mary Armstrong (11)
Otterhampton Primary School, Bridgwater

A Nerve-Racking Night

People waking,
Because the ground is shaking.

Making noises,
Like thundering horses.

A radiant light,
Breaks the night,
Of its sudden snoring!

A hair-raising creature,
At my bedroom door.

I scream for Mum,
But she just thinks,
Oh, never mind, I'll just ignore!

I smelled the dust,
Silhouetting round.

Then I tasted it,
And the last thing I remember,
Was a slimy face touching my finger . . .

Sophie Austin (9)
Otterhampton Primary School, Bridgwater

Rockets

Rockets zooming in the sky,
Way up high,
Zooming past,
Very fast,
They're very loud,
They go past a cloud,
The booming of the engine,
The roaring of the engine,
The men inside,
Way up high,
In the sky!

Billy Scotting (8)
Otterhampton Primary School, Bridgwater

Out Of This World

Today I went out of this world,
I floated up sky-high,
I drifted into the galaxy,
And reached the moon by night,
The world around me felt comforting,
I had mixed opinions inside,
As I sat silently alone,
Watching the world go by,
Today I went out of this world,
I floated up sky-high,
I drifted into the galaxy,
And reached the moon by night,
As everything started to become quiet,
I sat sadly crying alone,
Living in space is really cool,
But sometimes I wish to go home.

May Bruckel (10)
Otterhampton Primary School, Bridgwater

Space Aliens

I dreamed a dream of aliens,
I cannot tell you why,
But in my dream I saw the huddle
Go hastily grabbling by.
They moved beyond Uranus,
They made their disgruntled journey
Through the street of dropping jaws,
They moved on green and gooey claws.
I watched the stars above
Glistening and gleaming,
But when I looked back down again
They were gone, completely gone.
I dreamed a dream of aliens
It's just a bit weird though.

Harry Payne (11)
Otterhampton Primary School, Bridgwater

The Galaxy

I wonder what it's like in space,
Jumping over Mercury while saying hello to the sun,
Standing on Venus is quite a sight,
Earth is where I've always been but still the best planet,
Sitting on the moon is the best view of them all,
Mars is red as blood, next door neighbour is Jupiter,
Jupiter, second biggest of them all, his poor little Saturn sitting all alone,
I sit down on the ring of Saturn watching the pale planet,
Uranus and Neptune, blue as the sea, colder than the North Pole,
As I go over the last planet they call Pluto, I see the sun,
Illuminating all of space,
I woke up in my bed, in my house on Earth,
I dreamed a dream of space,
I cannot tell you why,
But I went slowly floating by.

Freddy Perham (9)
Otterhampton Primary School, Bridgwater

I Dreamed A Dream Of UFOs

I dreamed a dream of UFOs,
I cannot tell you why,
But in my dream they were quickly shooting by,
Leaving the stars behind.

They jumped right onto Mercury,
And sprinted over to Mars,
They skimmed the top of Jupiter,
And flew down to the stars.

I dreamed a dream of UFOs,
I cannot tell you why,
But in my dream they were quickly shooting by,
Leaving the stars behind.

Amelia Cadmore (10)
Otterhampton Primary School, Bridgwater

Bright And Colourful

Bright and colourful,
Out of this world,
Shiny stars,
All of that whirl,
Solar system,
Lollipops,
Aliens erupting,
Sweetie shops,
Big, bright moon,
Powder explosions,
Into the unknown potion,
Bright and colourful,
Out of this world,
Shiny stars,
All of that whirl.

Olive Jean Maidment (10)
Otterhampton Primary School, Bridgwater

Why Are There Stars In The Sky?

I wonder why there are stars
In the sky
Why, oh why?

You see them at night,
But not by light
Why must they disappear?
If I could touch them they would be near.

I wonder why there are stars
In the sky
Why, oh why are there stars
In the sky?

Abrianna Wood (11)
Otterhampton Primary School, Bridgwater

Light Of Blindness

Light-slinger
Slow walker
Bright-giver
Sight-burner
Gun of brightness
Dart of light
Glance of blindness
Wave of darkness
I say goodbye until tomorrow
But until then, bye bye . . .

Rhys Smith (9)
Otterhampton Primary School, Bridgwater

A Dream Of Starships

I dreamed a dream of starships
I cannot tell you why
But in my dream I saw the squadron
Go fast zooming by
Blasting asteroids like mad, dust emerged from under
They all shot through the dust
I stood there stunned under the moon
I dreamed a dream of starships
I cannot tell you why
But in the dream I saw the squadron fast zooming by.

Austin Doble (10)
Otterhampton Primary School, Bridgwater

OUT OF THIS WORLD - South West England

My Night In Space!

I went to space last night,
I stayed awake the whole time!
Hmmm, let's see, I . . .
Jumped on Jupiter,
Floated past Mars,
Stood on Saturn's ring and chased the stars,
I raced to Uranus and met an alien,
Then alone I sat on the sun,
Space is cool . . . But Earth is way more fun!

Grace Bennett (11)
Otterhampton Primary School, Bridgwater

Unknown

I'm mysterious
I'm unknown
I'm future tech

Whoever sees me
Will pay
I'm pitch-black

I'll make you scream
Who am I?

Henry Wood
Otterhampton Primary School, Bridgwater

Meeting A Martian

5, 4, 3, 2, 1, ignition! The roaring monster shot through the air,
The astronauts were living beyond their dreams,
But when they got to Planet Mars,
They heard a piercing scream,
'A Martian,' the poor men cried.
'Come on! I want to go home!'
So they left the fat, red Martian,
Upset, annoyed, alone.

Alexandra Mockridge (10)
Otterhampton Primary School, Bridgwater

The Solar System

Neptune is as blue as the beautiful sea.
Jupiter is as big as it can be.
Uranus please you shouldn't forget.
Saturn has the brightest ring, I bet.
Mars isn't as tasty as you think.
Venus is more beautiful than the colour pink.
Mercury is the first of them
And that completes our solar system.

Harry Philip Pyke (9)
Otterhampton Primary School, Bridgwater

Fireball

A flashing ball playing in the sky
Like a diamond in the high
Flashing ball, flashing high
How I wonder what you are.

A ball of fire
Up so high
Shooting through the night-time sky.

Matthew Forrest (9)
Otterhampton Primary School, Bridgwater

What Planet Am I? Kennings

Blood planet.
Robot-covered.
8 years.
Life expected.
Chocolate name.

What am I?
(A: Mars).

Jack Shand (10)
Otterhampton Primary School, Bridgwater

A Dream Of Spaceships

I dreamed a dream of spaceships
I cannot tell you why
But in my dream I saw the ships go blasting by
I dreamed a dream of spaceships
I cannot tell you why
But in my dream I saw the ships go blasting by.

Charlie Turner (9)
Otterhampton Primary School, Bridgwater

I Dreamed A Dream Of UFOs

I dreamed a dream of UFOs, I cannot tell you why.
But in my dream I saw them gently hovering by.
They hovered past my window.
They hovered through the night.
They didn't leave until the alien had waved
Goodnight!

Tom Brooks (9)
Otterhampton Primary School, Bridgwater

Comet

Zooming in outer space.
A flaming rock in the darkness.
An astonishing sight to see.
A splash of colour in the sky.
A comet heading straight for Earth.
Argh!

Kieran James (9)
Otterhampton Primary School, Bridgwater

Circle Of Space

Sparkling comet roaring past,
Circling the Earth, Jupiter and Mars,
So many planets that haven't been found.
With rings of ice and bits of stone,
Open the sky light, look out far,
Watch the rockets go zooming past.

Sam Webber (9)
Otterhampton Primary School, Bridgwater

Pluto

P urple planet in the sky
L ook up above the world so high
U p high is where you will find
T he planet Pluto
O verwhelming with joy.

Amelia Chloe Abina Williams (9)
Otterhampton Primary School, Bridgwater

OUT OF THIS WORLD - South West England

The Universe

All the planets in the large universe
Saturn, Jupiter, Neptune and Mars
These are all incredible stars
Rotating for 24 hours, let's call it a day
Of all the things to say, let's say we support Earth.

Oscar Stone (8)
Otterhampton Primary School, Bridgwater

Team GB!

T umbling our way down the long runway
E very member has a part to play
A thletes need to stay on top while
M andeville and Wenlock are mascots

G ymnasts, rowers, archers and wrestlers
B ritish Olympians are never restless

T riathlons, cyclists of running fame
E xcellence is the name of the game
A rchers, shooters take your aim
M edals come at the end of the game

G reat Britain rules the Mexican wave
B MX velodrome or mountain slave

T eams of cyclists win again and again
E nter taekwondo, boxing and the judo ring
A im high to take the bling
M arathons of 26 miles we run

G ames for all, enjoy the fun
B ars and beam take us to the extreme

So there we have it, Team GB!

Kitty Stone (9)
St Aldhelm's CE(VA) Primary School, Shepton Mallet

45

Out Of This World

O ver the moon I see astronauts jumping everywhere.
U nder the stars I sit.
T he planets are spinning around.

O ver the sun and back again.
F riends are good to go to space with.

T he moon is as bright as the sun.
H ere we are, we are on the moon.
I magining there were 14 aliens on the moon.
S cience is a good thing to learn.

W aiting for the sun to wake me up.
O ver the stars I go.
R ockets are amazing.
L ights of the moon.
D ying to see stars go by.

Trinity Hazel Piper Legresley (10)
St Aldhelm's CE(VA) Primary School, Shepton Mallet

Out Of This World

O verwhelming rocket ship.
U ranus cartwheeling around the cosmos.
T he sun in all its glory.

O verlooking space.
F oggy mist spraying out from the rocket.

T he amazing stars like diamonds.
H appy faces waiting for the rocket's departure.
I can see everything.
S hooting stars gliding through the galaxy.

W eightless.
O ut of this world.
R umbling rocket.
L onely planets orbiting the sun.
D amp puddles lying around on Pluto.

Luke O'Brien (9)
St Aldhelm's CE(VA) Primary School, Shepton Mallet

Out Of This World

O ut of the atmosphere,
U nderneath the stars,
T he planets are spinning.

O n with the universe,
F laming fumes.

T racking for a place to land,
H earing a space shuttle,
I magining how it will be,
S mokey smog.

W hizzing through space,
O ne small step for Man,
R acing around each planet,
L ighting up the sky,
D ancing on the moon.

Ayishah Parrott (10)
St Aldhelm's CE(VA) Primary School, Shepton Mallet

Out Of This World!

O ur spaceship facing the shining sun.
U p and up we go through space.
T he stars, each and every star looks small.

O ver the moon is darkness and little specks of light.
F rom planet to planet we go.

T he size of the different planets I see.
H uge asteroids whizz by.
I think they must be the size of small planets.
S eas of blackness are the most I can see.

W hipping along we move.
O ily smells are in the rocket.
R ushing stars pass.
L ong strides I take as I run on the moon.
D uring this, there was a gentle puff of stars exploding.

Daniel James (10)
St Aldhelm's CE(VA) Primary School, Shepton Mallet

Bilbo Baggins' Adventure

Once there was a hobbit
Who lived in a hole
He had a pet mole.
He went on a weird adventure
And found himself a troll.
He was nearly the cook
But then the dwarves came
And got the book.
Then they found some goblins
And they got the robins.
They found a secret door
With a key on the floor.
Then they looked at the dragon
Who lay on the floor.

Noah Robert Dowding Lees (8)
St Aldhelm's CE(VA) Primary School, Shepton Mallet

Supernova

My fuel is running low,
I will burn out just like so,
My flames are getting small,
Soon they'll be nothing at all.

My gravity is getting strong,
In a few minutes I'll be gone,
I might die with just a hiss,
Or it might go something like this.

I just feel like sighin'
I'm the next to be dyin'
I think I must do something soon,
Because I probably might go,
Boom!

Cameron Fernandez McEwan (10)
St Aldhelm's CE(VA) Primary School, Shepton Mallet

Wolves

Wolves can be in any pack
They fight all night
And never go back.

Some are bad, some are nice,
But they never go to sleep
At night.

Most are horrid, some are kind,
But what would they do
At morning rise?

Did you think to look behind you
Because I think something is
Going to frighten you.

Molly Connock (9)
St Aldhelm's CE(VA) Primary School, Shepton Mallet

Dogs!

Dogs are cute
You need to pick up their poop
Dogs are full of energy
You have no excuse.

Dogs are colourful
Although they like to play
Sometimes they feel ill
So you need to treat them all day.

Dogs like food
They eat, eat, eat
Because of my dog
I never get to sleep.

Phoebe Evans (9)
St Aldhelm's CE(VA) Primary School, Shepton Mallet

What Am I?

Sea-swimmer
Passenger-carrier
Cargo-transporter
Horn-blower
Steam-belcher
Anchor-dropper
Water-glider
Country-visitor
Life-saver
Dock-waiter.

A boat.

George Milton-Parry (9)
St Aldhelm's CE(VA) Primary School, Shepton Mallet

Out Of This World

P arallel universes waiting to be found.
L ighting up the star-encrusted sky.
A scending out of Earth into space!
N ew planets yet to be discovered.
E xcellence all around me, amazing, it's true.
T he cosmic comets, parading proudly.

E arth, wonderful water covering its surface.
A mazing astronomy strikes again!
R ising above the swirling solar system.
T he blinding flashes of a supernova.
H earts that make up Planet Earth, are the most amazing of all!

Danniellé Pittard (9)
St Aldhelm's CE(VA) Primary School, Shepton Mallet

Astronauts

A liens are out of this world
S weating hands
T rusting team
R ocket science
O ur universe
N ASA, the company
A stronauts go to space
U niverse
T he sun shining bright
S hooting stars.

Grace Chapman (10)
St Aldhelm's CE(VA) Primary School, Shepton Mallet

What Am I?

Awful-joker,
Good-runner,
Crazy-driver,
Football-player,
Mad-maker,
Bad-swimmer,
Fantastic-cuddler,
A great winner,
But all these things make a . . .

Summer Kearn (9)
St Aldhelm's CE(VA) Primary School, Shepton Mallet

The White Snowman

I am freezing
I live in snow
I have a carrot nose
I have button eyes
I have a hat

I have sticks for my arms
I am white like snow
I am excited because I am newly made
What am I?

Alana Fiddy (8)
St Aldhelm's CE(VA) Primary School, Shepton Mallet

Out Of This World!

S himmering shiny stars,
T housands of stars light and white,
A mazing angelic atmosphere,
R oaring rockets raging through space,
S un burning hot as if it was a volcano,

M arvellous mounds for miles and miles,
A dventures among every planet,
R ed and orange the planet glows,
S izzling surface under my feet.

Archie Biggs (10)
St Aldhelm's CE(VA) Primary School, Shepton Mallet

Giraffes

I am a giraffe in a scarf,
What a laugh!

I am a giraffe in a skirt,
What a laugh!

I am a giraffe that likes dancing,
What a laugh!

I am a giraffe in a park
What a laugh!

Scarlett Way (8)
St Aldhelm's CE(VA) Primary School, Shepton Mallet

What Am I?

Cute-cuddler
Heart-warmer
Happiness-spreader
Fierce-fighter
Noise-maker
Speedy-sprinter
Hug-giver
Piercing-predator.

Charlotte Mary Pole (8)
St Aldhelm's CE(VA) Primary School, Shepton Mallet

What Am I?

Coal-chewer
Steam-giver
Toot-tooter
Light-sparker
Speedy-darter.

I am a train.

George Robert Durston (9)
St Aldhelm's CE(VA) Primary School, Shepton Mallet

What Am I?

Blood-sucker,
Fast-runner,
Meat-eater,
Head-breaker,
Kind-shiner,
Loud-whistler,
Great-hearer,
Speedy-chaser.

Georgia Moon (9)
St Aldhelm's CE(VA) Primary School, Shepton Mallet

A Land Animal

I like gazelles
But they're in cells
I have spots
But they're like dots
I am yellow
I can bellow
I am the fastest land animal.
What am I?

Hayden Evans (8)
St Aldhelm's CE(VA) Primary School, Shepton Mallet

What Am I?

Happiness-giver
Chat-chatter
Kind-protector
Good-helper
Joy-bringer
Smile-provider.

I am a friend.

Libby Sawyer (9)
St Aldhelm's CE(VA) Primary School, Shepton Mallet

Jupiter

J upiter, the biggest planet of them all!
U nique stripe and beauty.
P lanet Earth is the only planet with life on it!
I nto outer space I blast!
T he aliens are closing in on me!
E ntering the rocket I was so ecstatic.
R unning on Jupiter, well that was hard!

Jack Gilham (10)
St Aldhelm's CE(VA) Primary School, Shepton Mallet

The Giant Whale

A whale with a long tail,
A whale in a mood, also very rude,
A whale is very long, also sings a song,
Also very long, but not that strong,
A whale with a very long tail,
A whale with a snail, a whale that is pale.

Katherine Dyke (8)
St Aldhelm's CE(VA) Primary School, Shepton Mallet

Aliens

A liens are out of this world.
L ighting up the solar system.
I magining how it will be.
E arth is where humans live.
N ASA is a famous company.
S pace is where the astronauts are.

Liam Kennedy (10)
St Aldhelm's CE(VA) Primary School, Shepton Mallet

Out Of This World

P laces you have never been.
L and like flowers in the air.
A nxiously waiting
N erves staring.
E cstatic to be there.
T errified of the heat.

Evie Ward (9)
St Aldhelm's CE(VA) Primary School, Shepton Mallet

Space

S hining stars above me.
P reparing to land on the moon.
A liens playing hide-and-seek
C aptain commanding to come home.
E xcited journey I had.

Emma Witcombe (10)
St Aldhelm's CE(VA) Primary School, Shepton Mallet

The Spider

Can see as well as a hideous black cat in the gloomy dark
All the girls are scared of me
I make webs of silk
I have fangs so sharp and like to suck your blood
My eyes are boulders staring at you.

Stefan Olindraru (8)
St Aldhelm's CE(VA) Primary School, Shepton Mallet

Dads

Dads are fun,
My dad makes me laugh,
He embarrasses me when a friend comes round,
He's a crazy dancer,
My dad is so funny.

Billy Sheppard (8)
St Aldhelm's CE(VA) Primary School, Shepton Mallet

Out Of This World!

M issing home already, it's like I've been here for days.
O rbiting planets as colourful as a million rainbows.
O n my own, feeling as lonely as a one person party.
N o, I've had an amazing time here but unfortunately
    it is time to go home as every astronaut has to.

Lily-Mae Beatrice Sealey (10)
St Aldhelm's CE(VA) Primary School, Shepton Mallet

I Love Doves

D oves in love
O ne lovely dove
V ery pretty
E very lovely dove!

Lola Pittard (8)
St Aldhelm's CE(VA) Primary School, Shepton Mallet

Baby Bats

B ats are cute, and find the truth,
A re mice your favourite treat?
T ake your flight, and make a sight,
S tretch your wings and find the glistening king.

Fern Nathan (9)
St Aldhelm's CE(VA) Primary School, Shepton Mallet

Taekwondo - Haiku

Taekwondo is great,
Kicks and punches keep you fit,
This sport makes you strong.

Jack Burgess (9)
St Aldhelm's CE(VA) Primary School, Shepton Mallet

The War

On the train going into war
Happy times I seek in my head
I know war is near
Clouds of thick, black smoke
Comes towards me
I hear gunshots in the distance.

In the trenches
Cold and frightful
Trenches all around
I start shooting and I can't stop
Tons of German soldiers
Falling to the ground
Crash
Then I got shot
Blood was racing out
At a hundred miles an hour
My heart stops beating
And I fall to the ground.

Amy Joanne Hunt (10)
St Andrew's CE(VA) Primary School, Weymouth

Butterfly Dream

Silent wind battering at the break of dawn,
Out of a chrysalis,
Out in the big wide world
As colours fill the sky.

Beauty as it might be,
Danger is round the corner,
Short life doesn't matter
As colours fill the sky.

Wings as picturesque as a picture,
Body is like a twig,
But as delicate as a petal
As colours fill the sky.

Nevertheless the view is astonishing,
Flowers have never grown more,
Glowing brighter than ever
As colours fill the sky.

Butterfly dream,
A dream that never fades.

Ruby Measures (10)
St Andrew's CE(VA) Primary School, Weymouth

OUT OF THIS WORLD - South West England

Fantastic Food

Food is really yummy,
Please don't eat it all,
And please don't rock the plate,
Otherwise it will fall!

Cereal is important,
You can eat it every day,
Once you've eaten your cereal,
You can go and play.

Ice cream can be colourful,
It can come in different flavours,
But the best thing about ice cream,
You can even have it with wafers.

Apples are very healthy,
They count as your five-a-day,
If you keep on eating sweets,
Your teeth will just decay!

Bethan Phillips (10)
St Andrew's CE(VA) Primary School, Weymouth

Space

Creative storm of black,
As I walk through,
The shimmering stars twinkle,
But what is that?

It's the alien from Planet Mars,
Or Jupiter,
It's the unknown keeper,
Of all in space.

It's the Milky Way,
The galaxy,
The solar system too
And the gates to open the mystery to space.

Mae Rodia (9)
St Lawrence CE Primary School, Lechlade

I Need To Go Home

I need to go home,
Back to Planet Mars,
I'm all on my own
And there are no cars,
To go home to Planet Mars.

I need to go home to Planet Mars,
To Planet Mars,
To Planet Mars.

I need to go home to Planet Mars,
I can't jump on stars,
But it's not that far
To go home
To Planet Mars,
To Planet Mars,
To Planet Mars.
I need to go home to Planet Mars.

Tosca Knight (9)
St Lawrence CE Primary School, Lechlade

The Moon

Neil Armstrong was the first,
To travel to the moon,
To see the wondrous
Silver stars,
So close to Planet Mars.

Swirling galaxies,
Circling him,
No blue skies
And fluffy white cloud,
Instead pitch-black skies
And galaxies.

Emily Tinney (10)
St Lawrence CE Primary School, Lechlade

Space

Stars sparkling in the dark
Showing me the way to Mars
But instead the rocket took me to Saturn
Next to Mars.

In front of me is a black hole
I'm scared, what is going on
Help me please, anyone in space
Can you save me?
I'm being sucked into the dark hole.

Isobel Parker (10)
St Lawrence CE Primary School, Lechlade

Space!

Space is black,
With little shining stars,
A twinkling ball of fire,
Is really far.
I need to go home now,
All the way to Mars,
Neptune is blue,
With crystal-blue rock,
A shining ball of blue.

Emily Coe (10)
St Lawrence CE Primary School, Lechlade

What I Can See In Space

Mix with a sprinkle of stars
Is a thought of zooming cars
That is what I can see in my rocket made by me
How beautiful the sea of space can be
The line of planets
Dazzling round the sun
Follow its master, the sun
The stars surrounding them like students
I just can't wait to tell my mum!

Scarlett Rodia (9)
St Lawrence CE Primary School, Lechlade

To Pluto We Go

Far away from the sun
Far away from fun
Listening for life out there
Listening for noise out where?

Black darkness crackling away
Hoping you would play
Now you are on the planet
Just looking at the sunset.

Campbell McDiarmid (10)
St Lawrence CE Primary School, Lechlade

Untold Mysteries

The creature's body is a thick sea of black,
Its coat of stars makes me want to turn back,
The helmet of planets, the heart of all suns,
A vortex in each hand lights up the night stars.
A door of creation unravels a mass of untold mysteries
To find and unwind.

Aloula Goymer (9)
St Lawrence CE Primary School, Lechlade

Out There In Space

My mind has opened,
To a thought,
What is out there,
Among the stars,
A deep black sea,
Of mysteries to see,
I swear a life form is waiting,
Waiting there for me.

Esme Barlow (10)
St Lawrence CE Primary School, Lechlade

Space

I leave Earth without a trace
Into a world of black
I fly up to space
But I want to go back
I jump back into my rocket
I can't go back home
Another planet I meet
I'm stranded all alone.

Brooke Etty (10)
St Lawrence CE Primary School, Lechlade

Space!

Stars that are small,
Planets that are cool,
Nine planets all about,
Weird things creeping me out,
Twinkling shines,
What can I find?
The sun is bright,
Giving us light.

Olivia Peach (10)
St Lawrence CE Primary School, Lechlade

Space Mysteries

Deep sea black,
Silver stars a-twinkle
The planets form a line to see the giant
Who rules them all
The Milky Way adrift
None has explored
Beyond the entrance to unknown mysteries.

Olivia Cripps (10)
St Lawrence CE Primary School, Lechlade

Space - Cinquain

Space rules
There is no sound
If you don't look around
There are lots of galaxies here
Space rules.

Jago James (10)
St Lawrence CE Primary School, Lechlade

Janet On Mars

Yo, her name is Janet,
She lives on a planet,
Called Mars,
Which has no cars,
So she said, 'Dang it!'

Daniel Graham (10)
St Lawrence CE Primary School, Lechlade

As I Landed On The Moon

As I landed on the moon
I saw a giant spoon.

I also saw some moon rocks
They smelt like my stinky socks.

Then I saw Mars
When I brought some chocolate bars.

As I saw an American flag
That was wrapped up in a bag.

Then I saw a rocket
That appeared up in my pocket.

Then I saw a star
That unusually had a giant scar.

Just as I saw the sun
He ate a giant bun.

Later I went to Saturn
That had a colourful pattern.

Owen Heaney (9)
St Thomas More RC Primary School, Cheltenham

Up, Up And Away

Up, up and away
From Earth and beyond
The rocket will sway
Between Earth and Mars
Will there still be shooting stars?
From up there I'm surprised to see cars
As I went past Saturn we all enjoyed the pattern
Poor old Pluto on its own so far away
Unfortunately, my rocket is made of clay
I saw a satellite flying by but never got to say goodbye
When I go to space I'll ask that thing to slow its pace.

Christopher Neale (9)
St Thomas More RC Primary School, Cheltenham

Up, Up And Away We Go

Up, up and away we go
Higher than a UFO.

Up, up and away we go
I am feeling nauseous.

Up, up and away we go
I am feeling happy.

Up, up and away we go
I can hear my radio.

Up, up and away we go
I saw an alien.

Up, up and away we go
I saw an ugly alien.

Up, up and away we went to Mars
To go and find shooting stars.

Up, up and away we go.

Kayla Young-Collins (9)
St Thomas More RC Primary School, Cheltenham

On My Way To The Moon

On my way to the moon
I saw a planet
It was a colourful planet
It was a colourful, living planet
It was a colourful, living, artistic planet
It was a colourful, living, artistic, spooky planet
Then I saw aliens
They were angry aliens
They were angry, fierce aliens
They were angry, fierce, man-eating aliens
Then they disappeared
What will happen next?

Brandon Njengah (9)
St Thomas More RC Primary School, Cheltenham

Up, Up And Away

Up, up and away I zoomed
Into space and I kept the pace

Shooting stars
Past Mars

As we landed on Saturn
We admired the pattern

Up in space
I slowed down the pace

As I landed on Mars
I looked at shooting stars

Up, up we go
The mission control said go slow.

Kaitlyn Booth (10)
St Thomas More RC Primary School, Cheltenham

Who Am I?

Alien-creator
War-winner
ET-inhabited
Volcano-minefield
Spaceship-makers
Astronauts scared
Exploration
Aliens
Lava-covered
Earth's buddy
Nowhere's muddy
Two moons
I am Mars.

Joe Taylor (9)
St Thomas More RC Primary School, Cheltenham

Mars Is Cool

Up, up and away we went
To Mars to see the shiny stars.

Up, up and away we go
I saw a UFO.

Up, up and away we went
To space to the base.

Up, up and away we went
To Mars to find shooting stars.

Sonny Street (10)
St Thomas More RC Primary School, Cheltenham

Who Am I?

Alien-maker
War-creator
Volcano field
ET home
Red planet
Ice water
Fourth planet
Alien armageddon
War-winner.

McCauley Ayres (9)
St Thomas More RC Primary School, Cheltenham

OUT OF THIS WORLD - South West England

On My Way To Space

On my way to space
I saw a dark green alien
It was an angry alien
It was an annoying, angry alien
It was an ugly, annoying, angry alien
It was a creepy, ugly, annoying, angry alien
And he wanted to chase me.

Kay Mary Piper (10)
St Thomas More RC Primary School, Cheltenham

Neptune

Neptune where the wind blows cold.
Zombies on there never get old.
Neptune where everything is frozen.
Icicles hang like sharp, shiny daggers.

Riley Sibthorpe (10)
St Thomas More RC Primary School, Cheltenham

Mars

Mars is beautiful
Mars is bigger than the moon
Mars is really hot
I am Mars!

Emily Jayne Piper (10)
St Thomas More RC Primary School, Cheltenham

The Tom Boy

Pink and flowery,
Towers of Malory,
Lipstick, powder and paint,
Girlie, whirly, really swirly,
All these things I ain't.

I'm scruffy, I'm dirty,
I'll never wear skirties,
You'll never catch me in a dress,
Mud and germs and lots of worms,
I'm always in a massive mess.

Stealing honey from bees and climbing trees,
These are the things I live for.
Playing with spiders, making mud sliders,
Then crashing in through the door.

Riding my bike and being a tyke,
Not playing with dollies and bears,
But one of the things I really don't like
is girlies plaiting their hair.

Now writing is fun and swirly,
Words are forming so fast I might pop,
But writing a poem is girlie,
So being a tom boy, I'll stop.

Katie Bartlett (9)
Stockland CE Primary Academy, Honiton

My Pet Human

When I landed on Earth,
It was different to Planet Glight,
Not cold and not dark,
But warm and so bright.

A few minutes passed,
A girl human I met,
I could take her to Glight,
And she'd make a good pet.

I asked with a smile,
'Would you come home with me?
We could go on long walks,
And my planet you'd see.'

She answered, 'I will,
But there's things I must know,
Are you all slimy as slugs,
And do you all glow?'

I said that we did,
Because Glight is so black,
Then we hopped in my spaceship,
In a zoom we were back.

Phoebe Wakley
Stockland CE Primary Academy, Honiton

Planets

I would like to see the planets
I think the planets would be fun
I would like to see the sun as well
I could go there with my mum
We could go to Mars and see the stars
We could see Saturn and its rings
Flying around the planets
We could see lots of pretty things.

Isabella Corp-Hill (7)
Stockland CE Primary Academy, Honiton

Walking Butterflies

There were two beautiful butterflies
They were perched on a slippery seat
Sunning their wings in the burning heat.
Suddenly, *whoosh,* they fell straight onto the floor
And lost both wings, oh how sore!

Up they jumped and realised that they couldn't fly
Oh my!
Sizzling sausages, what shall we do?
So they tried to walk, it worked, they could walk.
'We have to find the butterfly fairy to fix our wings
Even though it will be scary.'

Into the woods they went
Trying to find the beautiful butterfly fairy.
They had to walk for one whole hour to get there
What a nightmare!
But there she was with her magic words
'Zip, zap, zing, make their wings appear in a bling!'
As quick as lightning their wings did appear.
No more walking for the two beautiful butterflies.

Saffron Doble (7)
Stockland CE Primary Academy, Honiton

Playing Cricket

I'm playing cricket and I struck the wicket.
I bashed the ball and hit a six
The ball landed with a crash and smashed
So I had to fix.
I bowled the ball and hit the target
And everyone shouted
'You hit the wicket!'
The ball came low to me and I caught it
And everyone shouted, 'Howzat!'

Jonathan Elliot Triner (8)
Stockland CE Primary Academy, Honiton

OUT OF THIS WORLD - South West England

Disco Land

Once there was a spaceship flying high,
It kind of looked like a pie,
It entered a multicoloured land,
Apparently it was called Disco Land.
It sounded like there were cakes everywhere,
Everyone gets their share.
There are multicoloured people,
No one gets fat,
There isn't a single bat.
Absolutely no one is sick,
No one is angry,
There are candy cane trees
And there are no peas.
There are pale blue houses,
There is a disco floor,
No one does a single chore.
The sky is purple,
And at night the sky sparkles and shines,
There are some fabulous signs!

Liberty Wheeler (9)
Stockland CE Primary Academy, Honiton

My Dog Florence

Florence likes swimming at the beach,
Florence likes digging at the beach,
Florence loves the beach.

Florence likes running with her bone,
Florence likes burying her bone,
Florence loves her bone.

Florence likes playing with her friends,
Florence likes chasing her friends,
Florence loves her friends
But most of all, Florence loves me.

Edie Martin (9)
Stockland CE Primary Academy, Honiton

Pants Pirates

Once upon a time there was a poem called Pants Pirates.

P ants Pirates are very mischievous and naughty
A nd they always go up to people and chop your pants
N o one can attack Pants Pirates because they are too powerful
T he naughtiest pirates in the world are the Pants Pirates
S pying on people is a very good rule for Pants Pirates

P arrots are the Pants Pirates', look out
I nside the treasure chests are lots of golden pants
R aiding ships is very important because
   you can steal people's treasure
A nd their ship was called Long John Silver
T heir favourite food is roasted boxer beef and gravy
E pic pants have been missing across the world
   and it has been reported on the news in every country
S o every morning check your pants to make sure
   there are no Pants Pirates.

Isaac Parris (7)
Stockland CE Primary Academy, Honiton

I Saw A Star

I saw a star, but was it that far?
So I jumped in my rocket, the size of a pocket.
As I got closer, I was as hot as a toaster.
Then, I realised I was at the sun!
The sun reminded me of my warm and beloved mum.
Then, as quick as a flash I was off which made me cough!
Just before noon, I landed on the moon.
With a whoosh and a push, I jumped out onto the dust,
I peered around but there was nothing to see.
But suddenly, there were lots of eyes staring at me!
Should I run or could this be fun?
What would you do?

Phoebe Grace Lovell (9)
Stockland CE Primary Academy, Honiton

OUT OF THIS WORLD - South West England

Heroic History

H eroic history is my poem's name
E gyptian mummies all look the same
R omans are fierce warriors and have big shields
O ne day in 1914 , First World War began on the battlefields
I ncas built huge cities from massive blocks of stone
C ountries such as Britain dropped bombs
　　on the German city, Cologne

H uge dinosaurs like the diplodocus were longer
　　than two buses end to end
I n AD72 the mighty Colosseum was built that went around a bend
S anta Maria was the leader of Columbus' fleet
T he Greeks surprised the Trojans, a horse with big feet
O ne step on the moon for Neil Armstrong in 1969
R ed-bearded Viking named Erik with armour that's so fine
Y ears flash by at the speed of light showing many different times,
　　then it gets to now.

Is history really that fast?

George Parris (9)
Stockland CE Primary Academy, Honiton

What Is Beyond The Universe?

It could be death,
Your imagination, or even
Your wildest dreams,
Or the land of custard creams.
Maybe it is the land of salty breath,
That needs a whip of the finest sensation.
We just don't know what is beyond the universe
But perhaps someday in the future we will.

Sofia Corp-Hill (9)
Stockland CE Primary Academy, Honiton

Max The Martian

Max the Martian munches on Mars
When he eats chocolate,
He prefers it in bars.
When he has lemonade,
He likes to have it in a glass
And when Max has a picnic,
He sits on grass.
When he does run he comes first
And when he has a sack race
He is the worst.
Sometimes he goes to a cave,
And has a sunbathe.
What a good day it has been.
On Tuesday, my good lad,
I wish I could see the cows moo,
And the crows crow
And Max mow the lawn.

Rose Moorman (7)
Stockland CE Primary Academy, Honiton

What's Up In That Sky So Dark?

So what is up in that sky so dark?
Jumping Jupiter is like a jet shooting through the sky.
The sun is sitting on Saturn weaving her silk threads.
Venus the colour of violet is in a very vile mood.
Pluto, like a Disney character, is a party popper,
And my final favourite is marvellous milkshake making Mars.
So that's what is up in that sky so dark.

The Hawkins (8)
Stockland CE Primary Academy, Honiton

Spring

I love the sight of beautiful lambs,
Bouncing in the meadow,
Chicks run around eating bugs and slugs,
Spring,
Spring,
Spring,
I say hello to the lambs,
They baa back at me,
I say hello to the chicks,
They cheep back at me,
I love the sound of the blue tit's song,
Tweet, tweet, tweet they go,
I love the flowers,
I love the flowers
In the morning breeze,
I just love spring, the sound of spring,
Spring, spring, spring.

Tabitha Millington (7)
Stockland CE Primary Academy, Honiton

My Mud Pies

My mud pies are marvellous but messy.
My mum moans, 'Maisy, your mud pies are mayhem.'
I measure my mess in Mum's moans.
My mugs of milkshake are magnificent muddy masterpieces.
My muffin mixture is mashy, muddy mayhem.
My madras is a mixture of muddy meat, mint and moss.
There is no maximum to my mud pie making.

Maisy McCollum (8)
Stockland CE Primary Academy, Honiton

Flexablazia

Once lived Flexablazia,
Who was urged to enter a gym competition.
But when she got tangled, Flipperboy said,
'I will help you on one measly condition.'
Flexablazia, curious, looked him up and down.
Flexibility wasn't her favourite noun.
'I'll do anything!' poor Flexablazia cried.
'Then stretch further for me!' and over she flied.
Flipperboy watched with a smile on his face
And smirked like he thought he was totally ace.
Because Flexablazia didn't know the extent,
She twisted and stretched, but too far she bent.
Poor Flexablazia, for whom we all cry,
Suddenly snapped, and yes, she did die.
My tragic story has come to an end,
Goodbye to you, my precious friend.

Minnie Zarri (10)
Stockland CE Primary Academy, Honiton

OUT OF THIS WORLD - South West England

Yummy Mummy And Delightful Daddy

Life-savers they are,
They bought us a seven-seater car,
I love them dearly,
Yours sincerely . . .
The daughter of Mama!

They teach me to love, to live,
Don't hide from myself, to give,
Take chances - they teach me,
Observe rules - be friendly,
The daughter of Papa!

A family home they have made,
I know I'll thrive - not fade,
Educating me for sure - they are pearl-pure,
It's true, it's actual, everything is satisfactual!
Anna.

Anna Keen (10)
Stockland CE Primary Academy, Honiton

My Similes

Polar bears are as white as snow.
Snowflakes are as beautiful as diamonds.
Stars are as bright as bright brilliant bulbs.
Aliens are as sloppy and green as the king snail of Greenland.
The moon has holes as big as a mine.
The sun is as hot as boiling fire.
An owl is as noisy as a plane or train.
A house is as still as a rock or a pot.
Best friends are as pretty as a flower.
Leaves are as colourful as a rainbow.
The clouds move around as much as people.
Poison is as deadly as a bite from a crocodile.
A walnut tree's trunk is as wide as a hedge.
A table is as breakable as a tree.
Rabbits are as cute as a teddy bear.

Kate Alexandra Cook (8)
Stockland CE Primary Academy, Honiton

Innocent Alien

O n and on the spaceship went,
U p and up we flew,
T ime ticks by so slowly

O ur minds were sleepy too
F ar away from Earth now

T he passengers were anxious
H arry (my little bro)
I s even crying so
S pace is really fun, don't get me wrong

W andering aimlessly, I think I spot an alien
O h my gosh, is this a trick?
R evealing itself more and more
L eaving green slime behind it
D ivine and shimmering it drifted away, what can I say?

Molly Ann Yasmin Young (10)
Warden Hill Primary School, Cheltenham

OUT OF THIS WORLD - South West England

I Went To Space

I packed my case,
To go to space.
I wonder what I will see?
Maybe a trace,
Of an alien face,
Come along with me.

We will go in a rocket,
It's pink, don't mock it!
I won't charge you a fee,
Close the door and lock it,
The key is in my pocket,
We will also have some tea.

We will drive some cars,
When we get to Mars,
Sounds good, don't you agree?
We will use some jars,
To catch some stars,
I hope I get more than three!

We went to the sun,
To have some fun,
I fell and hurt my knee.
We had to run,
Because we were done,
It was far too hot, you see.

I used the phone,
To call back home,
But they could not hear me.
We're in the ozone,
And I can see Rome,
We have to land in the sea!!

Ella Newman (7)
Warden Hill Primary School, Cheltenham

Baby Joe

Baby Joe, my little brother,
Went to space with my mother.
He was young, still did not care,
'Bout going to space with no hair.

My mother, you see, was very brave
And wanted to show her husband, Dave.
Then at last she could be,
The heroic one in t' family.

Eventually they appeared close to Mars,
From there they could see tiny cars.
But then the dreaded time had come,
To feed the little baby's tum.

His terrible, messy eating habits,
Were the reason we had rabbits.
They ate up all the yucky grub,
So we didn't have to clean it up.

Now the ship was full of dirt,
And poor Mum was purely hurt.
With no shower to wash her face,
She drifted away from the human race.

Thankfully, the journey came to an end,
With angry Mum driven round the bend.
He ruined her chance of being a star,
So now she hadn't gone very far.

Sienna Viveash (10)
Warden Hill Primary School, Cheltenham

OUT OF THIS WORLD - South West England

It Wasn't Me Miss!

'Why did you do that, John?
Do tell me why.
Why did you do that, John?
You made Billy cry!'

'I didn't do it, Miss.
Don't blame me!
I didn't do it, Miss,
Can't you see?'

'Why did you do that, Bob?
Do tell me why.
Why did you do that, Bob?
You made Billy cry.'

'I didn't do it, Miss!
Don't blame me!
I didn't do it, Miss,
Can't you see?'

'Why did you do that, Billy?
Do tell me why.
Why did you do that, Billy?'

'The truth is, I did!'

Becca Allen (9)
Warden Hill Primary School, Cheltenham

Way, Way Up In The Sky

Way, way up in the sky,
Higher than you could ever fly,
Among the stars and planets too,
The moon is always looking at you.

Way, way up in the sky,
Higher than you could ever fly,
While you're looking at flaming-hot Mars,
You're surrounded by bright, twinkling stars.

Faye James (10)
Warden Hill Primary School, Cheltenham

In Space!

This is space, space, space,
It's so ace, ace, ace,
Space has got a very good pace, pace, pace,
For some reason I'm tying my lace, lace, lace,
In space, space, space.

Space is really fun,
It's full of stars, hun!
No one can explain,
How it doesn't rain!
In space, space, space.

Aliens fly around, around, around,
Making us spin round, round, round,
Some are really small,
Others are really tall,
In space, space, space.

Space is very dark,
It makes us wanna bark!
Space is really high,
In the blue sky!

Sam Danson (10)
Warden Hill Primary School, Cheltenham

Swaps

'I'll give you a
Milky Way for a
Piece of hay
My favourite vest
Or my pretty dress
And all the rest
I'll give you £1,000
If you give me a Lamborghini.
Deal?'
'Nooooo!'

Jack Tomkins (9)
Warden Hill Primary School, Cheltenham

UFO Invasion On Earth

U nderwater creatures in the deep blue sea
F un on this planet for you and me
O ut of space aliens coming to a planet, but which?

I nto the planet that is now dark as pitch
N umbering the planets one by one
V owing that the aliens will have fun
A liens coming to invade from up above
S un shining from the middle giving out love
I nto a black hole, into the darkness
O nto the spaceship, the spaceship of starkness
N ow the planet is blue and green again

O ut from space it never looked the same
N ow what planet did they choose?

E arth is the answer but a lion never loses
A liens have invaded Mercury, Venus, Earth and Mars
R unning around them are the stars
T hat is the reason they got invaded
H ooting owls have now been raided.

Kate Mitchell
Warden Hill Primary School, Cheltenham

Comets And Stars

C omets fly through the sky
O ut of this world like a fly
M ars and Jupiter, out of space
E arth is also all of our base
T hey're all out of space I say.

S tars are everywhere
T ake your chance up there
A liens live in this place
R eptillian-like is the wee alien's face.

Alwyne Adrian Williams (10)
Warden Hill Primary School, Cheltenham

Red Balloon

Mercury, Venus, Earth and Mars,
Surrounded by pretty stars,
Jupiter and Saturn,
We'll go there soon.
Flying in our red balloon,
Uranus and Neptune,
So close yet far,
We could try and get there in our car,
We could try and get there in our bus,
As long as the passengers don't fuss.

Mercury, Venus, Earth and Mars,
Eat your moon cheese beneath the stars,
Carried by our red balloon,
It's time to go home quite soon.
Our time is very soon to end,
We've now set the brand new trend.
Hopefully everyone will go to space
And learn that it's a magical place.

Scarlett Gracie Cave (10)
Warden Hill Primary School, Cheltenham

Outer Space

Oh, wondrous space,
It races with great pace,
At night we look up at a star,
That is something you wouldn't see in a tavern bar.
Maybe a comet,
You should watch it,
At an amazing speed,
These stars look down at our world of endless greed.
That ball of fire that is bigger than the sun,
It goes unnoticed just like when you run.
So they watch us, they always look,
But us, we just end up reading a book.

Matthew Haines (10)
Warden Hill Primary School, Cheltenham

OUT OF THIS WORLD - South West England

Space!

You go to space in a ship
When you get high Earth looks like a pip
If you land on the moon
You'll jump around like a balloon
Space is so high in the sky
Some planets look like tasty pie
Space has huge black holes
Which suck up evil souls
There are one million stars
Surrounding Planet Mars
The ship started floating down
Then my face had a huge frown
I was leaving planet space
I was going back to a normal place
Suddenly, I saw some ground
Then I heard a massive pound
Then I saw some astronauts
Well that is what we all thought.

Daniel Edward Robertson (10)
Warden Hill Primary School, Cheltenham

Space

G reat times you can have in space
A lthough a rocket is your base
L asers fired by a droid
A little chance to be crushed by asteroids
X ylophones cannot be heard
Y ou're too far away from Earth

R obots!
O uter, outer, outer space
C omets shooting in your face
K arate cannot save you now
E legantly riding a rocket, wow!
T remors echo all around.

Jack Nathan Pope (10)
Warden Hill Primary School, Cheltenham

How An Alien Came To Earth

He cannot fall at a later date,
Coming down in a ball of fire,
The alien's fate,
Appears to be dire.

Planets of rock and lava,
Came spinning past,
The world is getting steadily darker,
The stars are fading incredibly fast.

Then, out of the blue,
The alien crashed,
Onto something with a dark blue hue,
His life-support vest is nearly smashed.

A strange white thing comes whizzing through,
Cutting apart the H2O,
If it has spotted him, he has no clue,
And his instinct tells him to very swiftly go.

Thomas Davies (10)
Warden Hill Primary School, Cheltenham

The Magic Of Space

Rockets blast up in the sky,
Higher than a dragonfly.
To find out more about space,
Because it is an unknown place.

Astronauts float on the moon,
In the blazing afternoon.
Stars are shimmering in space,
Giant comets quickly race.

While they are on the moon,
They feel like a big balloon.
What is this place?
It's outer space!

Bethany Browne (9)
Warden Hill Primary School, Cheltenham

Oh Jake!

Oh, the bravest of them all was Jake,
Who travelled to outer space.
Oh, what a silly boy was Jake,
Powering his rocket with cake!

Oh, Jake, what will we do
If a black hole swallows you?
Oh, Jake, will you go *zoom,*
Or will the rocket and you go *boom*?

Oh, Jake, you silly boy,
You really know how to annoy!
Oh, Jake, you'll never get out of the atmosphere,
(Or even lift this rocket here!)

Oh, Jake, ten seconds till you go,
But you really don't know . . .
Oh, you'll be known as silly boy Jake,
Powering your rocket with cake!

Katherine Toner (9)
Warden Hill Primary School, Cheltenham

Swaps

'I'll give you -
A plastic whistle,
A piece of chewing gum,
A pencil case,
A table,
A tree,
A building,
A kangaroo,
A cruise ship or the world.
How about that?
Deal?'

'Ummm - no!'

Antonio Bailey (9)
Warden Hill Primary School, Cheltenham

Space, Space!

Go into space,
This is the place,
Where you can go to Mars
And pass shooting stars.

Go into space,
This is the place,
Where you soar in the sky,
Whilst comets fly.

Go into space,
This is the place,
Where you see the sun
And the bright stars come.

Go out of space
And have a race,
Back home,
Whilst having a groan.

Millie Cunningham (9)
Warden Hill Primary School, Cheltenham

My Visitor From Outer Space!

There once was an alien who lived in space
I found him on a planet, it was a very strange place
The ground was red, the Earth looked green
It was the most beautiful sight I'd ever seen
Then out of nowhere I heard a strange sound
So I turned around to look at the ground
And there I saw a tiny, green alien lying on the floor
It was so cute
I wanted to sing him a lullaby on my flute
I finally decided to take my new friend to my house
I told him to be as quiet as a mouse
To this day he's still my best friend!

Laila Khaira (8)
Warden Hill Primary School, Cheltenham

OUT OF THIS WORLD - South West England

Earth And Space Parting . . .

The astronaut slipped on his heavy, white suit,
Then heaved on an enormous, platinum boot.
He made sure the air was working in his socket,
Then looked down at the stairs up to the rocket.

Now stepping into the spacious metal room,
Would this be a dream or a scary doom?
Lifting on the helmet and funny-looking tubes,
He thought about eating food from small cubes.

Staring around, starting to fiddle with the costume,
This new little astronaut tried to assume,
That blast-off would be in the next heartbeat,
as he started to lift up from his seat!

Now he could hear the 10-1 countdown,
Looking out of the window, he could barely see the town.
Everything went shaky and a funny noise started!
As the distance between Earth and space . . . parted.

Faith Warrington Alder (10)
Warden Hill Primary School, Cheltenham

The Earth And Stars

The Earth spins all around and round,
So silent, not a sound,
Mercury, Venus, Earth and Mars,
Sparkling as a glamorous star.
Never stops and always spins,
Round and round,
'It's time for bed,' my mother said.

Loops and loops and loops of stars,
Never ever lose their shine,
The pretty, beautiful, golden stars,
Glared at the beautiful view of space.

Aamena Toufique Qureshi (10)
Warden Hill Primary School, Cheltenham

Comets All Around

C omets whirling all around,
O rnate views all around,
M eteors passing by,
E arth seems so far away,
T he training that got you here,
S tars you see every night,

A stronauts in space,
L ife is different there than here,
L ovely space that surrounds you,

A ll the bright stars you can see,
R ain on Earth you'll never feel,
O ver Earth you go,
U ranus is so far from here,
N ever could you be happier,
D own you go back to Earth.

Rebecca Maughfling (10)
Warden Hill Primary School, Cheltenham

OUT OF THIS WORLD - South West England

The End Of The World!

There was a boy whose name was Jim,
Who always forgot everything.
He forgot to do his homework and even go to school,
And always fell into every swimming pool!

His mum was a weirdo, his dad was a farmer,
And even they knew how to stay away from lava.
He was so forgetful (or maybe even worse),
His dad warned him so much that one day he might burst!

Now it comes to the day where Jim was going to die,
Everyone panicked and even the birds couldn't fly!
Only ten seconds to spare, would Jim be in time?
He rode his bicycle as fast as he could, 'Come on everybody, let's fly!'
Everyone else made it, except Jim,
Because he was forgetful no one could stop him!

Zara Sharaf (9)
Warden Hill Primary School, Cheltenham

Day Poem

I come every morning, to brighten up your day
I let you see and I shine over Earth like a blanket
Every summer I heat up and let children have fun with shadows

I can sometimes hide behind clouds but I will always come back again
I'm as hot as fire and I'm a sphere shape
If you are cold I will warm you up.

Sophie Miles (8)
Warden Hill Primary School, Cheltenham

Planet Teachers

Mrs Marsh from Mars,
Mr Ring from Saturn,
Miss Juniper from Jupiter,
Mrs Milk from the Milky Way,
Mr Galex from another galaxy,
Miss Vene from, you guessed it, Venus,

But our headmaster, well I've just got started!

Tabitha Murray-Birks (8)
Warden Hill Primary School, Cheltenham

A Different World

S tars glittering in the sky
P lanets circling in space
A stronauts whizzing off to the moon
C omets whirling around the galaxy
E ndless space in every direction.

Hannah Maughfling (8)
Warden Hill Primary School, Cheltenham

Please Mrs Jones

Based On 'Please Mrs Butler' By Alan Ahlberg

'Please, Mrs Jones
This girl, Kady
Keeps taking my pencil, Miss
What shall I do?'

'Swallow it if you like, love
Flush it down the toilet
Put it up your vest, my lamb
But don't ask me.'

'Please, Mrs Jones
This girl, Kady
Keeps copying my work, Miss
What shall I do?'

'Go sit on the roof, my love
Go do your work in your locker
Do your work up the tree, darling
But don't ask me.'

'Please, Mrs Jones
This girl, Kady
Keeps stealing my grapes, Miss
What shall I do?'

'Go hide your grapes up your nose
Go and eat your grapes in the sewer
Just don't ask me!'

Taylor Ilott (9)
Warden Hill Primary School, Cheltenham

Please Mr Krug

Based On 'Please Mrs Butler' By Alan Ahlberg

'Please, Mr Krug
This boy, Jeff Spug
Keeps stealing my tennis ball, Sir
What shall I do?'

'Kick him in the leg
Hide behind a tree
Throw it over the fence, boy
Do what you think best!'

'Please, Mr Krug
This boy, Jeff Spug
Keeps stealing my football, Sir
What shall I do?'

'Burst it with a pin
Flush it down the loo
Throw it up a tree, boy
But just shut up!'

Edward Churchman (8)
Warden Hill Primary School, Cheltenham

On The Carpet

Based On 'Please Mrs Butler' By Alan Ahlberg

'Please, Miss Smith, this boy Billy Brooks
Keeps taking my whiteboard, Miss
What shall I do?'

'Just take a seat, dear, and listen to me.'

'Please, Miss Smith, this boy Billy Brooks
Keeps taking my seat, Miss
What shall I do?'

'Just kick him on the floor or push him in the chest
Just don't ask me!'

Jessica Taylor (9)
Warden Hill Primary School, Cheltenham

In Space

In space,
There is no case,
There is no pace.
The lights glow,
The spaceships flow,
The Earth floats.
I see the light,
I feel the daylight inside,
I'm holding it tight.
It's dangerous,
It's courageous.
There's so much time,
It feels like mine.
I have a soul,
There is a hole.
There are a hundred stars,
I see the lights
Which look like flashing lights
On a car.

Shenice Cooney (11)
Whipton Barton Federation, Exeter

What A Dream!

I was dreaming about space last night,
The moon's light was so bright,
It lit up the whole sky,
I had so much fun playing with the moon's monsters,
Until it was time for the moon to turn off the bright light.

Morning was coming,
My dream was fading,
The monsters disappeared,
And the light reappeared,
I wish my amazing dream was real.

Shelby Rose Tucker (11)
Whipton Barton Federation, Exeter

Alien Attack

Dark when ships come,
UFOs making us scream,
People screaming and crying,
Dogs barking,
Kids running,
Homes blowing up,
People getting abused,
Cats hissing,
Aliens blasting us,
Turning us into aliens,
Enormous creatures,
Lasers coming from the sky
Ink splatting at us,
Acting like humans,
Naughty for killing,
Slimy goo dripping from their mouths.

Cameron Thomas (11)
Whipton Barton Federation, Exeter

Space

Star, star,
Burning bright,
Twinkling in the strange blue light,
A comet falling,
Hot and angry,
A moon so cold,
A sun so old,
Yet when you stop,
Think,
Look up,
What do you see?
Space,
For space holds Earth for you and me,
And space holds day and night and glee!

Alex Crane (11)
Whipton Barton Federation, Exeter

OUT OF THIS WORLD - South West England

The Comet

Bang, crash, boom!
Bang yells the comet, kicking his legs.
Fire emerging, more and more burning.

Sizzling, he sprints towards the Earth.
He runs to his enemy, pushing anything
That gets in his way.

No one has a say what he does.
He does what he wants.
If you tease him, he will retaliate.

As he gets nearer and nearer,
A country field lies sleepy.
Corn lies weeping.
It comes closer and closer.

Bam!

Hope Oldridge (11)
Whipton Barton Federation, Exeter

Constellations

C areful craters
O minous voids
N umerous stars shine
S atellites spinning
T ravelling
E lectric black holes
L ovely rings
L ovely space rock
A nalyzing Earth
T he astronaut dives
I ntelligent life forms
O minous meteorites
N ine planets
S paceships fly through the sky.

Lewis Moore (10)
Whipton Barton Federation, Exeter

101

Out Of This World

O utstanding, amazing space is great
U nderstanding the world out there
T he quest that never ends to find answers

O ut of this world
F or the astronauts who have conquered the moon

T he planets and the moons
H ow the planets turn and rotate
I t's incredible how we reach the atmosphere
S ome amazing universe to look upon

W hen it's gone
O ur lives will disappear as if we were never here
R eturning life as a non-existence
L ovely planets are in our solar system
D anger for future planets.

Taylor Murphy (10)
Whipton Barton Federation, Exeter

Astronauts

They're brave
They float
They might have a goat
They have been to space
Do you have an ace?

They're in a rocket and nothing can block it
In space, meat they crave.

They're brave
They float
They might have a boat
They have been to space
A very large place.

They're in a rocket that nothing can block
In space, meat they crave.

Callum Harris (12)
Whipton Barton Federation, Exeter

OUT OF THIS WORLD - South West England

Spaceman!

It was a moonlit, bright sky,
When a spaceship came flying by.
A shooting star came past with its very bright light,
The astronaut was not going to put up without a fight.
As an alien was about to bite,
A meteor came flying by
And knocked out the alien,
Goodbye.
The astronaut was happy,
He had a very bloated tummy.
It was a little bit funny
Because he ate a bunny.
His family was a little bit worried,
When they Skyped him last Monday
With a satellite telly.

Alicia Louise Farmer (10)
Whipton Barton Federation, Exeter

Billy The Alien

Billy was an alien
From Sillzork
Out of the Milky Way
When people saw
They said, 'No way, Hosay.'
He was rejected
At the beginning
But one family
Saw his big heart
Billy loved his new home
But he was homesick
He remembered what he used to say
'Someday, I'll go places!'
And he was correct
We do not know about the rest . . .

Louis Harry Watkiss (11)
Whipton Barton Federation, Exeter

Take-Off

Skies are blue
Planets are green
Space is most colourful
Like a rainbow.

Watch out for the falling meteor
But you might fall when you blast-off.
Boom! Boom! Boom!
Falling bombs
Watch out, it'll explode.

Shooting star like a gun
Make a wish before it's gone
Make it quick like a shark
3, 2, 1, blast-off.

David Hurford (11)
Whipton Barton Federation, Exeter

Shooting Star

Shooting star,
Falling star,
Burning with a light.

Shooting star,
Falling star,
Lighting up the night.

Shooting star,
Falling star,
What a sight to see.

Shooting star,
Falling star,
Grant a wish for me.

Charlie Helmann (11)
Whipton Barton Federation, Exeter

Space

Sky is blue, space is black.
I'm full of surprises.
But I can never be destroyed.
I make big and bad explosions.

I watch you travel and walk on the moon.
I am all of the planets combined.
I control all of the planets.
I am darker than you can ever be.

I control the sun and every world.
I am your world.
You can never escape me, I am your ruler.
I control the sun which helps all of the worlds have light.

Brandon Martin (11)
Whipton Barton Federation, Exeter

Shooting Star

S parking stars
H azardously flying
O ver the moon
O ver the horizon
T imeless aliens
I nterstellar space
N umerous stars
G orgeous galaxy

S atellite system
T otal darkness
A stronauts floating
R eaching high.

Katie Mitchell (11)
Whipton Barton Federation, Exeter

Space

Star light, star bright,
The night sky was lit,
A shooting star across the sky,
When a spaceship came by,
Out came some strange shapes,
Holding something that looked like plates,
The stars blinked,
The spaceship had vanished like dust,
A meteor came flying,
To reach where it wanted to be lying,
After that, he had peace and quiet forever,
Stars, sun and everyone had gone to sleep!

Megan Reed (10)
Whipton Barton Federation, Exeter

The Rocket?

What happened to it?
It got stolen by an awestruck alien.
What happened to it?
It got blown up by a shooting star.
What happened to it?
It got destroyed by a meaty meteorite.
What happened to it?
It crashed onto Jupiter.
What happened to it?
It got absorbed by the star-bright sun.
What happened to it?
My poor, sad rocket!

Keira Lamerton (11)
Whipton Barton Federation, Exeter

Oh Moon

Up very, very, very high,
Miles up into the sky,
You are so, so pretty, oh why?
Huge and shiny in the stars,
Oh look, is that Mars?

Rockets fly to you,
We want to know about you,
But we already know lots about you,
How much more is there to know
Oh moon?

Ryley Mortimore (11)
Whipton Barton Federation, Exeter

Out Of This World

Sand-burner
Heat-bringer
Fire-starter
Puddle-drier
Grass-grower
Light-shiner
Wood-shiner
Mood-setter
Life-giver
The sun.

Corey Madge (10)
Whipton Barton Federation, Exeter

Out Of This World!

Earth is green and blue
Round and split in two
Riding to the moon
This journey is too soon
Back and forth we go
This rocket is too slow
My sight is not clear
Up here
Black and white
Just like the night.

Adam Wilson (10)
Whipton Barton Federation, Exeter

Space Poem

The sky is blue
Space is black
Spaceships flying, they never crash
The space is full of shooting stars surrounding planets, mainly Mars
Stars shining, aliens shining, planets turning
The sun's coming down
The moon's coming up
It's morning now space, time to go to bed
It's going to be dark soon
Then you can do this all over again.

Ellie-Mae Coles (11)
Whipton Barton Federation, Exeter

OUT OF THIS WORLD - South West England

Astronaut

Bouncing on the moon
It was such fun
I even got on TV
For being the first one
In my rocket
Blazing hot fire shot out
As I shoot out of space
I look down at the Earth below
Gravity is lifting me up, up, up
Until I'm flying!

Lauren Sprague (11)
Whipton Barton Federation, Exeter

Aliens

Cold, dark, deadly
Green as a bogey,
Look through a gap
In my bedroom door,
Hissing as I wiggle and giggle
In my sleep,
My eyes begin to weep
As I wake up from my sleep,
As an alien ran down my lawn till dawn
And left before I got into its UFO.

Eloise Taylor (11)
Whipton Barton Federation, Exeter

What Am I?

Black and dangerous
Come in all sizes
Dust of planets
Around it are discs of material
It is strange and mysterious
And nothing can escape, not even light!

What am I?
I wonder?
I am a black hole.

Emily Dunn (11)
Whipton Barton Federation, Exeter

Space

No sound.
Darkness-generator
Star-lighter
Black hole-maker
Death-bringer
Always dark
Life-risker
Last frontier
Space.

Danielius Demjanovas (10)
Whipton Barton Federation, Exeter

OUT OF THIS WORLD - South West England

The Marvellous Moon

The moon is like a sun at night,
It is as silver as a five pence coin.
The moon is like a ghostly galleon tossed upon cloudy seas,
It keeps on sailing, sailing, sailing.
The moon was created when there was a boom,
Its ribbony rays trickle off it like a stream after it rains.
The moon almost has magical powers when it disappears,
And then suddenly appears from behind a grey object.
The moon is just marvellous, marvellous, marvellous.

Tomas Piskac (11)
Whipton Barton Federation, Exeter

My Little Star

I know that one day she will not glow,
That her presence will go, that I know.
Watching the hunter shoot the stars,
Flying to Venus, to Earth, to Mars.
Oh, how she wishes to be free,
From her star-shaped cage that she'll always see.
She's always been there since the day she died,
All dressed up in silver, 'I'm fine,' she lied.
Soon she'll die - my little star.

Chloe Boyce (11)
Whipton Barton Federation, Exeter

As Bright As The Moon

Light-bringer
Star singer
Children-wower
Wave power
Tide-turner
Eye-burner
Light-reflector
Star-collector
Astronaut explorer.

Ben Turner (10)
Whipton Barton Federation, Exeter

My Space Dream Last Night

I felt like I went to space last night,
The planets were spinning round and round,
And the world was turning upside down,
But I was still on the ground,
The moon was shining as bright as the biggest light,
The stars were twinkling in my eyes,
I woke up the next day and said to myself it was just a dream,
But under my bed a blinding beam of light,
Shone like my dream last night.

Lillian Sharland (10)
Whipton Barton Federation, Exeter

OUT OF THIS WORLD - South West England

Boom

The blazing hot rock flying through the sky,
Powerful enough to destroy anything in its path.
Dead stars are indestructible,
They target Earth until *boom!*
They create craters in the world.
A fierce ring round the rocks,
Chilling in space, just waiting,
For the perfect wake, just waiting,
Because they will go boom and it could be now.

Danny David Knight (11)
Whipton Barton Federation, Exeter

Space Is My Home

Shooting stars flying through the air,
Praying planets floating through space.
Magical moon shining and glowing.
Giant Jupiter guarding the world.
Ancient aliens giggling with laughter.
Magnificent Milky Way, tasty and yummy.
Yep, this is space.
It's our home.

Lois Bennett (10)
Whipton Barton Federation, Exeter

I Am The Moon

When the sun goes to sleep, that's when I appear,
The night sky is what I keep,
I will follow you in the car,
My brothers and sisters are the stars.
'I am the moon,' I say,
Just look up, you may see me there,
I'll give you a clue, I'll be staring back at you.

Michaela Shapcott (11)
Whipton Barton Federation, Exeter

Moon

Shade-bringer
Sleepy time
Night-bringer
Dark time
Mood-setter
Sun-takeaway
Pyjama time
Dream-maker.

Conor Alsopp (10)
Whipton Barton Federation, Exeter

Will He Ever Come?

Will he ever come into my sight?
Will he ever come and block my light?
Will he ever come again to see me?
His warm, white glow is what I long to see.
His gorgeous smile as he crosses my path,
As I say goodbye, his light-hearted laugh.
I count the years since I've seen his face,
The one with no sadness, not a trace.

Mylie Freestone (11)
Whipton Barton Federation, Exeter

Out Of This World Kennings

Night-lighter
Star-brightener
Sun-blocker
Crater-maker
Moon-lander
Hero-maker
World-shaker
The moon!

Coeinn Preston (10)
Whipton Barton Federation, Exeter

OUT OF THIS WORLD - South West England

Zombies

Z ealous creatures small and tall
O verweight, crazy and all
M ysteriously running to your door
B utchering people for fun
I ntensely killing everyone with a massive machine gun
E verybody wants to run even if they hold a gun
S illy zombies go away, it's starting to become day.

Ollie Blackmore (10)
Whipton Barton Federation, Exeter

Space Aliens

The ship crashed on a planet, a purple planet, a petrified planet, a putrid planet.
I walked and walked nowhere because it was dark, just dark.
The air was low and I walked and walked.
I sat, I fell, I woke up.
I saw aliens, I ran, I fell, I woke up.
I saw I was on the ship . . .

Emanuel Krystian Kolbuszewski (10)
Whipton Barton Federation, Exeter

Out Of This World

Planets are awesome
Shooting stars light up my world
The moon is awesome.

Planets orbit well
Shooting stars are luminous
The moon has whitened.

Chidera Melie (10)
Whipton Barton Federation, Exeter

The Sun Riddle

The planet is in a large galaxy
It never stops giving light
Even when it's not needed
People call it rock of light.

What am I?
Sun.

Lila Rose Watkiss (9)
Whipton Barton Federation, Exeter

Aliens Are Outside!

A t my door there's something there
L eaning in the bushes
I n the trees, watching, with red eyes
E ntering my house
N othing is outside
S omething is inside.

Michael Macleod (11)
Whipton Barton Federation, Exeter

Space

Mars planet
Poison breather
Dark place
Flowing dust
Quiet sound
Stars-wisher.

Aaron Harry Brealey (10)
Whipton Barton Federation, Exeter

Sounds Of Space

Boom goes the spaceship crashing into stars,
Wham goes the engine getting nearer to Mars.
Whoosh goes the comet flying past a satellite,
Beep goes the satellite sorting out a human flight.
Zap goes the laser gun shooting at the enemy.
'*Argh*,' shouts the enemy running to be free.

Yvette Louise Bogardis (10)
Whipton Barton Federation, Exeter

Out Of This World

S tars shooting through the empty space
P eople exploring new planets
A steroids crashing down to Earth
C an you see the silly aliens?
E verybody preparing for landing.

Oliver Purvis (9)
Whipton Barton Federation, Exeter

Black Hole

Black hole is dangerous
Black hole is mad
Black hole has a gravitational pull
Black hole will rip you apart
Black hole is evil!

Luke Pring (11)
Whipton Barton Federation, Exeter

I Wonder

I wonder what's there,
Black, dark and spooky,
The black hole,
Who knows what's there?
Who knows, who will find out?

Reece Passmore (10)
Whipton Barton Federation, Exeter

Out Of This World

S hooting stars around the world
P lanets are invaded
A liens come to attack
C ities cold and dark like a shark
E verywhere is abandoned!

Verity Jones Orr (10)
Whipton Barton Federation, Exeter

Space

S tars up high
P lanets that don't fly
A liens that are weird
C reepy and scary
E xciting missions await.

Ella Stone (10)
Whipton Barton Federation, Exeter

Out Of This World!

S hooting stars light the sky
P lanets revolve but never die
A ir is cold up high
C oming home is an astronaut's aim
E ntering the atmosphere is the end of the game.

AJ Turner (10)
Whipton Barton Federation, Exeter

Space

S hooting stars race across the sky like jets
P ale aliens flying in their rocket
A mazing asteroids floating like balloons
C ool Saturn floating like a balloon
E pic moon makes the night bright.

Tyriece Swift (9)
Whipton Barton Federation, Exeter

Out Of This World

S hooting stars flying through the endless space
P eople exploring new planets
A stronauts are ready to land on the moon
C an you see all the silly aliens?
E verybody preparing to take off.

Nadia Thomas (10)
Whipton Barton Federation, Exeter

Out Of This World

S pace is high!
P ilots can't fly!
A stronauts can and do!
C ommanders lead the crew!
E arth has disappeared, life is really weird!

Kelsey Grinney (10)
Whipton Barton Federation, Exeter

The Black Hole

The black hole is evil
With no care or being fair for planets.

It will demolish everything in its path,
So beware, planets, here comes the hole of destruction!

Riley Smith (10)
Whipton Barton Federation, Exeter

Stars And The Sun

Stars shine huge with meteorites
Skies showering the world with uncomfortable sounds
Black holes capture then release, but not here
Somewhere with fear.

Tj Smith (10)
Whipton Barton Federation, Exeter

Space - Haiku

People exploring,
Natural phenomenon,
Stars zooming around.

Kasmira Swift (11)
Whipton Barton Federation, Exeter

Out Of This World - Haiku

It is above Earth
Space is high up in the sky
Has no gravity.

Elysia Jade Kingdon (11)
Whipton Barton Federation, Exeter

Untitled

As I gazed above my head,
Twinkling dots pinned to a dark sky,
A hula hoop attached to a ball,
Litter in space believe it or not,
A bright light going down in the west,
Unfortunately not cheese lay far ahead,
As I lay in a bed,
Images of space were spinning round my head,
An alien popped by,
It said, 'Night, night.'
I smiled.

Alexandra Grace Ley (10)
Whitchurch Primary School, Tavistock

Rocket In My Pocket

I wish I had a rocket
In my pocket
Or maybe I could wear it round my neck like a locket
I might wear rings like Saturn
They would make a good pattern
And light up like a genie's lantern
I'd rub it for a wish
Then go
Swish
Up to the moon like a balloon
Do you think there are cars on Mars?
I'm not sure but I know there are
Stars on my ceiling
They give me a zoomy, spacey
Out of this world feeling.

Tal Pearson (6)
Whitchurch Primary School, Tavistock

Untitled

One day I went to Mars to see the stars.
I found a rocket in my pocket.
It burst into lots of tiny sparkles.
From up here I can see the moon.
It makes me turn into a crazy loon.
But what I like best.
Is to see the stars that sparkle.
I can only see out to space at night.
The stars, planets and moon shine so bright.

James Drew Waites (6)
Whitchurch Primary School, Tavistock

On The Moon

On the moon you can't help but float
I got here in my big red boat
I row and row into the cheese
But now I'm here, let me home please!

It's cold up here and I've forgotten my coat
It's time for me to turn around my boat
To go home in the warm and dry
Goodnight everyone, goodbye!

Sheldon Blake Higgins
Whitchurch Primary School, Tavistock

Stars

Giant balls of glowing gas,
Shine at night not day,
Little dots dotted around the Earth,
People wonder how they stay.

Space is a big place,
Stars shine, the sun glows,
But not everyone knows.

Sophie Mackenzie (10)
Whitchurch Primary School, Tavistock

Out Of This World

Out of this world there is a place called space,
There are lots of planets,
And they all have one face,
I think there are 9 planets,
Mercury, Venus, Mars, Jupiter, Pluto, Saturn, Earth, Neptune and Uranus,
Saturn has one ring around itself.

Niall (10)
Whitchurch Primary School, Tavistock

YOUNG WRITERS INFORMATION

We hope you have enjoyed reading this book — and that you will continue to in the coming years.

If you're a young writer who enjoys reading and creative writing, or the parent of an enthusiastic poet or story writer, do visit our website www.youngwriters.co.uk. Here you will find free competitions, workshops and games, as well as recommended reads, a poetry glossary and our blog.

If you would like to order further copies of this book, or any of our other titles give us a call or visit **www.youngwriters.co.uk.**

Young Writers
Remus House
Coltsfoot Drive
Peterborough
PE2 9BF

(01733) 890066 / 898110
info@youngwriters.co.uk